Bringing in a New Era in Character Education

Bringing in a New Era in Character Education

EDITED BY

William Damon

HOOVER INSTITUTION PRESS
Stanford University Stanford, California

The Hoover Institution on War, Revolution and Peace,
founded at Stanford University in 1919 by Herbert Hoover,
who went on to become the thirty-first president of
the United States, is an interdisciplinary research center
for advanced study on domestic and international affairs.
The views expressed in its publications are entirely those of
the authors and do not necessarily reflect the views of the staff,
officers, or Board of Overseers of the Hoover Institution.

www.hoover.org

Hoover Institution Press Publication No. 508

First printing 2002
07 06 05 04 03 02 9 8 7 6 5 4 3 2 1

Manufactured in the United States of America

The paper used in this publication meets the minimum requirements
of American National Standard for Information Sciences—Permanence
of Paper for Printed Library Materials, ANSI Z39.48–1984. ♾

Library of Congress Cataloging-in-Publication Data

Bringing in a new era in character education / edited by William Damon.
p. cm.
Includes bibliographical references and index.
ISBN 0-8179-2962-2 (alk. paper)
1. Moral education—United States. 2. Character—Study and
teaching—United States. I. Damon, William, 1944–
LC311 .B74 2002
370.11′3′0973—dc21 2002019813

Contents

Introduction

William Damon

GENUINE CHANGE IN a modern educational system usually takes place slowly, if at all; but we have seen one notable exception to this in recent times. With astonishing rapidity, education in the United States has ended its failed experiment in separating the intellectual from the moral and choosing the intellectual as its only legitimate province. From K-12 schools to college campuses, instructors are paying attention to students' values and are accepting responsibility for promoting students' character.

By no means is this an unprecedented approach: indeed, it is a return to the more comprehensive "whole student" agenda that American schools had dedicated themselves to during the first three centuries of education in this country. But during the middle and latter parts of the twentieth century, educators found themselves embedded in a highly specialized, secular, knowledge-driven, postmodern world. Most responded by concluding that the moral part of their traditional mission had become obsolete. Moral relativism was in, *in loco parentis* was out. The dominant view held that educators should promote critical thinking and tolerance which, amazingly, were not viewed as moral values, but rather as neutral, inert positions outside the contentious realm of value choices. This thinking was a misconception that caused so many readily apparent casualties among the young that it was bound to be abandoned sooner or later. Fortunately the correction has occurred surprisingly quickly. As we enter the twenty-first century, it is well under way.

As an advocate for this correction, I have glimpsed the change even at the federal government level, which typically reacts to rather than induces cultural trends. At the dawn of the Clinton administration, Secretary of Education Richard Riley addressed a conference of character educators such as me who were looking for ways to reintroduce moral messages into the K-12 curriculum. The secretary supported our aims, but in response to a question commented (I cannot quote him verbatim after all these years) that he did not see much role for the federal government or for public schools in such an endeavor, because children's values were a private matter that should be reserved for families and churches.

Three years passed, with widely noted media accounts of youngsters harming themselves and others through morally misguided choices. In his 1996 State of the Union Address President Clinton proclaimed that every school in America should teach character education. He said: "I challenge all our schools to teach character education, to teach good values and good citizenship." Secretary Riley's Department of Education established a program to support this idea. Four years later, in the presidential election of 2000, one of the major candidates (the winning one, in fact) frequently campaigned on a promise to promote character education in America's public schools—a pledge that he, now President Bush, has acted upon since assuming office by tripling federal support for the Education Department program. I have believed in character education for most of my working life, but I never thought that I would see it arise as a major campaign promise in a presidential election, or garner so much support at the highest reaches of government.

We have entered a new era in character education, marked by broad public acceptance of the idea and endorsements by top elected officials from both political parties. This is a good start, a window of opportunity that could stay open long enough to allow worthwhile efforts to enter. But all such windows eventually shut if the worthwhile efforts stall or get pushed aside by less serious ones designed only to take advantage of the trend. How can we bring in this new era in character education to make the right kind of difference to the young people in our schools and colleges? What are the principles and approaches that provide character education the solid foundation to sustain it now and in the future, so that it again becomes a lasting part of our educational agenda rather than merely another trend? What obstacles in our present-day educational system must we overcome, and what new opportunities can we create? The purpose of this book is to provide some beginning answers to these questions. The authors are among the most innovative thinkers in the field today, and in their chapters they offer original solutions unconstrained by the misconceptions that have derailed moral instruction in our schools.

Each chapter puts forth a unique perspective on what is needed in character education today, but at least two main themes run throughout the volume. The first is a consensus that fundamental moral standards must be passed along to the young and that educators at all levels bear a serious obligation to transmit these core standards to their students. The question of "Whose values are these anyway?"—in recent years the battle cry of those who would keep schools barren of moral guidance—is shown to be moot by several of the authors. They are our values, the "our" referring to the worldwide community of responsible adults concerned with the quality and very futures of the civilizations that their younger citizens will one day inherit. The second theme that emerges from this volume is a shared determination to get rid of sterile old oppositions that have paralyzed even some of the best efforts in this field over the past few decades. Many oppositions have gotten in the way and must be transcended by a more integrated, inclusive, all-encompassing approach if real progress is to be made:

Habit and Reflection

Most parents know that it is essential to raise children to act right *and* to exercise good judgment in complex or difficult situations. Every child deserves to acquire reliable habits *and* strong reasoning skills. Children who do not acquire this beneficent combination may become untrustworthy to themselves, despite whatever good intentions they may have; or, alternatively, they may become automatons susceptible to malevolent influences that they cannot screen or evaluate. Strangely, contemporary scholarly discourse draws lines between the aims of fostering good habits and clear reasoning about justice and other moral matters. The philosopher Bernard Williams[1] criticizes his own field for setting up a false opposition between virtue theory (virtues simply being the characterological consequence of sustained habit) and justice theory (which advocates a constant thinking through of procedures that create social contracts and their implications for fairness). Williams points out that there should be nothing incompatible about virtue and fairness. Any full moral life aspires to achieve both. Williams notes that the two moral aims share common enemies—hypocrisy, a self-serving tendency to rationalize inaction or compromise, and a willingness (or too often an eagerness) to pursue supposedly moral ends through immoral means.

Compounding philosophy's confusion, a quirk in the history of psychology sets habit and reflection in opposition. In the scientific study of moral development, the two dominant camps for the large part of the twentieth century were the behaviorist and cognitivist traditions (the psychoanalytic tradition remaining mostly outside of academia because of its sparse research base). Behaviorism emphasized the person's conformity to rules and the conditioning of habitual modes of conduct;

1. Bernard Williams, *Ethics and the Limits of Philosophy* (Cambridge, Mass.: Harvard University Press, 1986).

whereas cognitivists such as Piaget and Kohlberg emphasized the person's capacity for reasoning and autonomous judgment.

Dividing the person in this way may or may not serve the purposes of scientific study—that is a debate for another occasion—but it is an unmitigated disaster for education, which must in the end deal with all the components of the developing youngster. The incredibly fruitless opposition between habit and reflection has been transplanted from psychology and philosophy to realms of educational theory and practice, where it has polarized character education efforts for precious decades. It is time to move beyond this needless argument and take as our target of moral instruction the whole child—habit and reflection, virtue and understanding, and every system of judgment, affect, motivation, conduct, and self-identity that contributes to a child's present and future moral life.

The Individual and the Community

Much rhetoric has been wasted arguing about the locus of the moral sense that we try to cultivate in every child. Extreme positions proliferate all across the ideational landscape. Some hold that morality is essentially biological, deeply rooted in an individual's genetic code, with the implication that individuals are born with varying degrees of it. This position leaves us little to do educationally but spot the bad seeds and get out of the way of the good ones. Even the question of whether parents matter has been taken seriously in recent years. At the other extreme, some insist that all moral truth resides in the community, that excessive individualism is the root of our problems, and the task of moral educators is to promote cultural transmission and an awareness of our interdependence. Neither position gives much credence to the age-old ideals of personal conscience, noble purposes, or inspirational social action.

The supposed opposition between the individual and the community is a popular myth based upon degraded versions of culture theory. The idea is that Western morality (especially the American version) stresses individual rights and responsibilities, unlike the rest of the world (Japan is often cited as an example), where a communal orientation prevails. More serious anthropologists[2] know that all such notions exist everywhere. Indeed, how could any society survive without holding individuals accountable for their actions, recognizing and protecting their rights (at least to some extent), or establishing some communal sense of the common good? Societies certainly vary in how they balance and express these moral orientations, in the degree to which they emphasize one or the other, and in the cultural traditions that organize them, but morality is always a matter of individual transactions with communities, and children must be prepared both to learn from their social settings and to follow their own consciences when the need arises. For educators, morality means teaching common values as well as helping every child acquire the kind of personal moral identity that ultimately will sustain the child's moral sense in any situation—joyful or grim, inspiring or corrupting—that the child encounters in life.

The Secular and the Religious

In these days when public school districts are sued for allowing student choirs to sing hymns, when valedictorians are forbidden to use the word "God" in their commencement addresses, and when teachers are reprimanded for wishing students "Happy Holiday!" before school vacations (I have not invented these incredible examples), it must be noted that things were not always so in this country. For most of our history, public education did not distinguish between moral messages conveyed in a secular package and moral messages conveyed through stories and sayings from any one of the world's religious traditions. Far from banning every expression of religious sentiment, public schools recognized it (generally in a nonsectarian form) as one source of moral inspiration and guidance. Schoolbooks were full of uplifting moral, spiritual, and

2. R. Shweder, *Thinking through Cultures: Expeditions in Cultural Psychology* (Cambridge, Mass.: Harvard University Press, 1991).

religious ideas mingled with lessons designed to teach literacy, math, and whatever else children needed to learn. It was part of what I referred to earlier as the whole student approach that did whatever it could to foster character as well as intellect, goodness as well as knowledge, purpose as well as competence.

Starting with the Progressive Era, and throughout the remainder of the twentieth century, public education split the secular from the religious, adopting the former and rejecting the latter. This choice was spurred by pluralism and a well-intentioned desire to protect children whose families might not share the beliefs expressed. I do not dismiss such reasons: they are important in themselves, and all children should learn to understand and respect the civil liberties concerns that they reflect. But such matters always must be viewed in the perspective of an overall pedagogical agenda, which in turn must be tailored to how young people learn.

How do young people learn moral beliefs and values? This book provides sound answers to this question, answers based on careful scholarship rather than on unanalyzed fears or wishful thinking. Some of the insights shared by many authors in this book are (1) young people learn best through clear messages—moral relativism and ambivalence leave young minds cold; (2) young people learn from positive instances of exemplary behavior. A single shining, in vivo example of virtue is a more powerful teaching tool than scores of abstract "do not's"; (3) young people have active, curious minds that eagerly seek new knowledge. They are not especially fragile, and the real danger is in turning them off by failing to provide sufficient inspiration, not in disturbing them with harmful information; and (4) young minds have great intellectual flexibility—they are capable both of absorbing the traditional wisdom of their culture and of making smart choices for themselves when they need to.

I have never heard of a youngster being harmed by witnessing another person's expression of spirituality, even when the form of spirituality is highly unfamiliar to the child. On the contrary, young people usually are fascinated and moved by such expressions and the more foreign the forms, the more they are likely to find them interesting rather than disturbing. The civil liberties concerns about minority rights and the dangers of theocratic oppression are adult issues worth teaching at some point, to be sure, but not frontline issues for the moral instruction of young people, who need to learn far more basic lessons about core standards such as honesty, compassion, responsibility, respectfulness, and fairness. Adult-centered concerns should not be used as justification for censoring a unique and powerful source of positive moral inspiration from our public schools. It is time to open our public schools once again to moral ideas set in a variety of religious as well as secular frameworks as well as to students' free expressions of spiritual faith.[3] Young people need all the inspiration they can get.

The Chapters in This Book

Each chapter in this book points to directions that character education must take at this juncture and offers strategies essential for progress. Taken together, the chapters suggest a comprehensive approach for such progress.

Arthur Schwartz identifies the starting point of our new era: no longer is the distracting question "Whose values?" bogging down our character education efforts. That question has been settled by a consensus throughout our society—a widespread, tacit agreement that all children should acquire the core values of civilized living that responsible adults cherish. Now that we can stop wasting our time on unnecessary

3. Some key ideas that we wish to pass down to children require an appreciation of their religious roots in order to fully understand their moral significance. The work ethic comes to mind as one such notion. Without knowing the religiously inspired concept of *calling* (or, similarly, the classic root of the word *vocation*), work can be seen as simply a convention or a nuisance that is too often necessary. I have heard not only disgruntled workers but also distinguished social scientists portray work in this way. For the work ethic to be an inspiring invocation rather than a oppressive injunction, it is important to convey to youngsters its origins in the belief that one should use one's occupation to serve God and, by extension, one's fellow humans.

uncertainty, we can make progress on the more profound and difficult question of how we can pass these values down to the younger generation in ways that will elevate their conduct and their life goals. Schwartz has his own answers to this that are at the same time innovative and very old. His suggestions about reintroducing wise maxims in curricula and his examination of how honor codes should be used in our schools should be required reading for educators everywhere.

Following a theme introduced by Schwartz, Christina Hoff Sommers shows why it is relativism, not indoctrination, that threatens the moral development of young people in our time. She starts with an example of ambivalence toward the right or wrong of cheating, an example that would be amusing if it were isolated or bizarre. Unfortunately, as I have discovered in my own travels through every level of our educational system, Sommers has given us a revealing glimpse into a grave malignancy that threatens both the character of our students and the integrity of our academic institutions (more about this below). Sommers offers a classic vision of moral education that springs from the principles of Aristotelean and Augustinian philosophy that is corrective of the laissez-faire excesses fomented by Rousseau and his legion of modern-day followers. Sommers shows us the depths to which misguided ideas can take us and offers hope for the future by describing approaches that can lead us to a better way.

Education, like medicine, is a field of practice; but, like medicine, it needs a scientific base in order to weed out ineffective (or even dangerous) practices from beneficial ones. The subfield of character education has been establishing a scientific base for some decades, and Marvin Berkowitz provides us with an up-to-date account of it. Beyond his chapter's importance as a rare state-of-the-science statement of what we know from solid evidence, Berkowitz also makes several key points that reinforce the main themes of this book. He rejects the false oppositions that have riven the field, creating in the end a synthesis that should appeal to a wide swath of practitioners (theoreticians and philosophers are another matter—it is possible that they enjoy the arguments too much to fully accept any synthesis). Berkowitz also takes pains to spell out what we don't know as well as what we do know. This is valuable for two reasons: first, it speaks for keeping our pedagogical methods open to change as our scientific base expands; and second, it reminds us to be humble in whatever approaches we try. Humility is a virtue that character educators should aim to foster among students as well as to practice themselves.

Lawrence Walker also takes us through the scientific literature, but with a more particular purpose in mind. Walker makes the case for an approach based on actual human examples of moral excellence, an approach that Walker calls moral exemplarity. The advantages of this approach are similar in both science and education: it can resolve oppositions of the sort that Berkowitz and others find futile; and it offers a compelling, indeed captivating, way of incorporating all the elements of morality that make their way into a human life. The use of moral examples for scientific study and educational practice has been explored before, but Walker's powerful analysis goes beyond previous writings to reveal the promise and significance of such an approach.

Warriors ennobled by moral principle are one archetype of exemplars, and Nancy Sherman shows how stoic principles have shored up the resolve and conduct of heroic warriors such as Navy Pilot James Stockdale. Sherman's treatment of stoic philosophy is subtle and evocative. She shows how stoic principles, when fully understood, offer a moral manner of managing one's emotions in times of pressure. This makes for a unique, invaluable contribution to the moral education literature that generally avoids the problem of inner emotional control. Sherman also sees the limits of Stoicism, cautioning that an overly rigid version may lead to emotional coldness and detachment from the empathic side of moral response. Her own resolution—"Stoicism with a human face"—bears implications for character education far beyond the military settings in which she has worked.

Sherman notes that she began her service at the Naval Academy with a visit commissioned by a navy chaplain in the wake of a shocking cheating scandal. I accompanied her on that visit, and my impressions are still fresh in my mind. Here was a group of incredibly dedicated officers, faculty, and student-midshipmen torn apart by an enormous breach in one of the navy's proudest traditions, its esteemed honor code. How could such a thing happen? My personal conclusion was that the ethics behind the code, and the moral bases of rules against cheating, were not properly understood by students at the Academy, for the simple reason that they were not being carefully taught. I believe that Professor Sherman's ethics course went a long way toward rectifying this situation.

That is the good news. The bad news is that similar and worse problems are prevalent at schools and colleges across the nation. Almost everywhere, there is a lack of clarity surrounding cheating. In her chapter, Sommers describes the lack of clarity shared by faculty and students alike. Tests that faculty distrust or students dislike do not justify dishonesty as a form of protest. This is not a legitimate act of civil disobedience, in which a dissenter openly admits to breaking a rule and bravely accepts society's sanctions for it. This is instead a deceptive, self-serving, and furtive bit of behavior, a step down the path to personal irresponsibility. When teachers tell students that they can't blame them for cheating on any tests that are unfair or meaningless, or worse, when teachers urge students to cheat as a way of boosting teachers' performance ratings (as news reports, incredibly, have verified), this is moral miseducation. It is training students to become dishonest. No ideological position about testing, competition, or anything else can justify such a choice. If there were such a thing as educational malpractice, this would be a prime example.

Clark Power's discussion of a cheating incident in a school where he worked provides another illustration of the deeply entrenched confusion surrounding this moral issue. Students struggle to sort out the difference between cooperation and dishonesty. One young girl believes she is being an altruist in the image of Mother Teresa by sharing her work with a friend! Students need the guidance that can teach them respect for school codes but many teachers, Power writes, merely "facilitate [rather than] instruct . . . [and] ask questions [rather than] provide answers." Although Power is more sympathetic to this kind of teaching than I, his chapter offers a poignant account of how his own mentor, Lawrence Kohlberg, moved to a more sociological position toward the end of his life, adopting Durkheimian insights about establishing a structure of moral authority for moral education. In this more traditional vision, a teacher becomes an elder collaborator who transmits cultural wisdom. Power's designation of this approach as countercultural can only be seen as ironic. He notes, for example, that Western culture is open to change and thus often countercultural with itself. Passing Western culture along means communicating this dynamic spirit, not a bad way to orient the younger generation to the excitement of democracy. But the culture that Power really counters is the prevailing atmosphere of our public schools. Here Power is in closer agreement with the other authors in this book, all of whom seek to elevate the desultory moral atmosphere that too many students today encounter.

Amitai Etzioni's *Communitarian Network* has played a key role in creating a nationwide discourse among educators dedicated to character education and in bringing this discourse to the attention of policy makers long before the idea became politically popular. The network organized a number of influential conferences in the 1990s, including the early White House meeting that I referred to above. In his chapter for this book, Etzioni charts out the "communitarian position" on character education, a position that centers on (1) affirming core values, (2) promoting empathy within the child and of bonds of attachment between the child and others, and (3) imparting disciplinary standards that emanate from legitimate authority, but that also become part of the child's own internal set of chosen beliefs.

In line with other authors in this book, Etzioni deals with the question of "whose values?" by pointing out that moral values are not at all arbitrary ("Values do not fly on their own wings," he writes). Etzioni looks to social institutions such as the family, schools, voluntary associations, and places of worship for reference points regarding the values that we must pass along to the young. His position places schools squarely within, rather than apart from, their communities. Our schools never should have become the sheltered enclaves of expertise and over-specialization that resulted in their neglect of moral values and character for much of the past century. Etzioni reminds educators that cultivation of students' character is necessary even for the academic parts of their mission: "You cannot fill a vessel that has yet to be cast."

In her chapter, Anne Colby fights the good fight for reestablishing student morality and character as targets of higher education's central mission. When they first were founded, most colleges and universities dedicated themselves to fostering students' moral development, but as higher education has drifted toward increasing specialization and compartmentalization, the original whole student agenda has been discarded. Those who would recapture the old ground have met with great resistance. Colby takes on each point of resistance with unassailable logic, effectively demolishing every familiar objection that has been raised against character education at the post-high-school level. Colby's chapter will inspire and protect those in higher education who are bold and caring enough to concern themselves with students' moral lives, yet find themselves besieged by those who would keep the ivory tower knowledge-pure and value-free.

For the present volume, Irving Kristol has revised an incisive statement that he originally wrote during the 1970s,[4] the heyday of values-neutral approaches to moral education. His chapter reminds us that a child's individual development requires guidance from people and institutions with firm moral bearings. Like Sommers, he rejects the Rousseauian view, so prevalent in schools today, that the job of adults is simply to get out of children's way and allow intrinsic goodness to emerge naturally. Kristol points to the necessity of authority in any moral

4. Ryan K. and D. Purpel, *Moral Education: It Comes with the Territory* (New York: Basic Books, 1977).

educational endeavor. He uses the concept of authority advisedly. First, he explicitly refers to legitimate authority. Second, he distinguishes legitimate authority from the illegitimate extremes of authoritarianism and permissiveness. Kristol's insight here echoes empirical conclusions from scientific child psychology, which has found that, ironically, authoritarianism ("do as I say because I said so") and permissiveness ("do whatever you want") have similarly ill effects—training children to be irresponsible and incompetent—whereas the consistent exertion of legitimate authority ("here's the right thing to do, here's why, let's discuss it openly and come to a mutual understanding about it") is the surest formula for successful child rearing.[5]

Kristol also makes the point that authority and liberty are inextricably linked, indeed that liberty is not possible without a context of legitimate and predictable authority. For me, this is among the most important points in his chapter, because it is so little understood or appreciated by much of the educational community. It is the reason that some of us still have our students read Emile Durkheim, whose theory elegantly explicated the reasons why, as Kristol writes, "In the case of authority, power is not experienced as coercive because it is infused, however dimly, with a moral intention which corresponds to the moral sentiments and moral ideals of those who are subject to this power." To the extent that education is, as Kristol terms it, an "exercise in legitimate authority," an offering of moral guidance for developing minds, it is a force for both personal freedom and character building.

Looking to the Future with a Remembrance of the Past

The future directions pointed to by the authors in this book are based upon what we have learned from the past. Efforts at character education generally are well-intended, almost by definition, but good intentions

5. W. Damon, *The Moral Child* (New York: Free Press, 1990); W. Damon, ed. *Handbook of Child Psychology*, 5th ed., vol. 1–4 (New York: John Wiley and Sons, 1998).

have not always prevented them from being misguided. In my own travel, I have seen many mistakes by educators who sincerely want children to acquire virtue and moral understanding. I have seen skin-deep programs that ask students to do nothing more than recite virtuous words such as *honesty*, *temperance*, and *respect*, and the words do nothing more than pass in one ear and out the other. I also have seen adults promoting the very behaviors that they are warning children against. Much like Sommers, I have heard teachers suggesting to students that it is all right to cheat on tests that seem meaningless. I have observed adults who counsel underage minors about alcohol abuse by telling them to stay within a one-drink-per-hour limit. I have seen teachers look the other way when students treat one another harshly or unfairly.

Such half-hearted messages mock character education. Children will neglect ideas that adults present superficially or ambivalently, and are brilliant at picking up subtexts. They love to explore the half-forbidden. Any instruction that begins "I'd rather not have you do this, but if you are going to anyway, be sure to . . ." is an irresistible invitation to give it a full-throttle try. The only way to dissuade a child from harmful behavior is through guidance that the child understands and takes seriously. The only way to stop cheating is to tell children that it's wrong, to explain why (it's unfair, it's untrustworthy), and to enforce the sanctions rigorously. The only alcohol and drug abuse programs that work—that result in less rather than more risky behavior—are programs that stress avoidance of these dangerous substances. But conveying don'ts to children can be only a small part of a successful character education program. Character education must have a positive side, a call to serve others and to dedicate oneself to a higher purpose. In the long run, it is a sense of inspiration that sustains good character. Commitment to a noble purpose can make learned prohibitions unnecessary. As they say in sports, the best defense is a good offense.

Charitable work is one way to introduce students to a larger purpose. Research has found that community service programs, especially when combined with reflection about the moral and personal significance of serving others, are powerful inducers of moral growth.[6] Spiritual beliefs, too, offer children positive intimations of transcendent purposes. Another transcendent purpose is the love of country and selfless dedication to it. In the case of a country that stands as a beacon of democracy and freedom, this is a noble sentiment. The common word for this sense of dedication is *patriotism*, a word that in recent times has not been welcome in many educational settings; yet now, when decent societies are called on to combat the evils of international terror, patriotism of the loftiest sort must resume its rightful place as a noble source of inspiration for our young. In order to wholly fulfill their character education missions, schools must open themselves to such sources of inspiration, becoming places where all students can discover their own moral callings and noble purposes.

6. M. Yates and J. Youniss. *The Roots of Civic Identity* (New York: Cambridge University Press, 1997).

Transmitting Moral Wisdom in an Age of the Autonomous Self

Arthur J. Schwartz

ALTHOUGH THERE REMAIN a few skirmishes here and there, the reports from the front lines are decisive: the battle over the question "Whose values?" has ended. For almost two decades this culture war has raged on, pitting a platoon of character educators, parents, and citizens against those (in schools and out) who are either highly suspicious or skeptical of the character education agenda. In the end, the primary stakeholders in our schools answered this thorny question for themselves: local educators, parents, and civic leaders came together in communities as diverse as Chattanooga and Chicago to reflect upon, identify, and affirm a set of core values. Even a cursory look at these lists reveals that moral principles such as honesty, compassion, and respect are the sorts of attributes that parents want their children to learn in school, practice every day, and cherish forever. With remarkable clarity and unity, schools and communities across the United States have put the "Whose values?" question behind them.

Today the debate has shifted to an equally thorny question: "How should educators transmit these core values to our children?" I use the idea of "transmission" purposefully, recognizing that the term has little contemporary currency, and for many conjures an extrinsic, cold approach to learning that deflates the agency of the student in the learning process. I disagree with this conception of the term "transmission" and I am going to make the case in this chapter that transmitting moral knowledge and ideals is essential for the moral health of our American society.

My sense is that we no longer use the term "transmission" because some fear it will lead us down a slippery slope to that most villainous of educational terms: indoctrination. Indeed, from Lawrence Kohlberg's seminal article "Indoctrination Versus Relativity in Value Education" in 1971 to Alfie Kohn's writings throughout the 1990s, scholars and progressive educators have worried that the real agenda of character education is to indoctrinate our children.[1] For example, in his 1997 *Phi Delta Kappan* article, Kohn writes:

> Let me get straight to the point. What goes by the name of character education nowadays is, for the most part, a collection of exhortations and extrinsic inducements designed to make children work harder and do what they're told. Even when other values are promoted—caring or fairness, say—the preferred method of instruction is tantamount to *indoctrination*. (429, emphasis added).[2]

Kohn is not alone in his sentiment. I do not believe I use hyperbole when I suggest that there remains a significant group of progressive educators and scholars who continue to fear that should the grip of character education ever take firm hold in our schools, our next generation of children will become blindly obedient to authority, patriotic to a fault—and worst of all—pious and religious.[3]

1. See Lawrence Kohlberg, "Indoctrination versus Relativity in Value Education," *Zygonu* (1971): 285–310.

2. Alfie Kohn, "How Not to Discuss Character Education," *Phi Delta Kappan* (1997): 429–39.

3. See Michael Apple and James Beane, eds., *Democratic Schools* (Alexandria, Va.: Association for Supervision and Curriculum Development, 1995); James Beane,

In order to prevent our schools from taking that perilously short stroll from transmitting values to indoctrinating students, progressive educators suggest that sovereign moral autonomy ought to be the endpoint of a moral education. Teachers should encourage young people to "author" their own moral constitutions. As Mark Tappan and Lynn Brown write: "In a very real sense students in a character education program are simply not encouraged to learn anything from their own moral experience, because such a program denies students any real moral authority in their own lives."[4] In contrast to the perceived dogmatism of character education, Tappan and Brown suggest that teachers ought to provide opportunities for students to reflect upon and tell their own moral stories (through poems, essays, plays, videos, and so on). By doing so teachers would be helping their students to "resist and overcome social and cultural repression" as well as to develop morally. Tappan and Brown concede that this emphasis and focus is rare in schools, but argue that it "would be even more difficult, if not impossible, to attain in an educational setting where all students are *indoctrinated* into a fixed set of traditional values, virtues, and rules of conduct"[5] (p. 199, emphasis added).

Putting aside the inflammatory rhetoric of personal liberation, I glean from the writings of progressive educators that students should be honest and caring *only* when these values constitute their moral identity.

Affect in the Curriculum (New York: Teachers College Press, 1990); Rheta DeVries and Betty Zan, *Moral Classrooms, Moral Children: Creating a Constructivist Atmosphere in Early Education* (New York: Teachers College Press, 1994); Deborah Meier, *The Power of Their Ideas* (Boston: Beacon Press, 1995); George Noblit and Van O. Dempsey, *The Social Construction of Virtue: The Moral Life of Schools* (New York: State University of New York Press, 1996); David Purpel, *The Moral and Spiritual Crisis in Education* (New York: Bergin & Garvey, 1989); Gregory Smith, *Public Schools That Work: Creating Community* (New York: Routledge, 1993).

4. Mark Tappan and Lynn Mikel Brown, "Stories Told and Lessons Learned: Toward a Narrative Approach to Moral Development and Moral Education," *Harvard Educational Review* 59:2 (1989): 182–205.

5. Ibid., 199.

This conception of moral identity focuses primarily on the authenticity of moral feelings and self-expression ("what feels good is good"). In addition, these educators repeatedly assert that something is terribly, terribly wrong if a student is honest or caring because these are the values that his or her parent, teacher, mentor, rabbi, or minister think important. The transmission of values from one generation to the next is dismissed by progressive educators as traditional or hegemonic or patriarchal in nature. In short, the moral umbilical cord must be severed cleanly and completely. Mikhael Bakhtin, a favorite theorist for many educational progressives, sums up this point of view when he writes: "[O]ne's own voice, although born of another or dynamically stimulated by another, will sooner or later begin to *liberate* itself from the authority of the other discourses" (emphasis added).[6]

As Alasdair MacIntyre would put it, this strident emphasis on attaining moral autonomy, liberation, and transformation (at all costs) is a "grave, cultural loss."[7] It seems odd to me that to gain autonomy or to "own" your moral voice means having to liberate yourself from the sources of your core values—parents, mentors, religion, or mediating institutions such as Scouting and sports. Even John Dewey, whose philosophy of education remains an inspiration and ideal for many contemporary progressive educators, understood the need for transmission of values. In his classic book *Democracy and Education* Dewey writes: "Society not only continues to exist *by* transmission, by communication, but it may fairly be said to exist *in* transmission" (emphasis added).[8] As Dewey suggests, the purpose of this chapter is to explore how vitally important it has been for each generation to transmit its moral wisdom to the next generation.

6. See Mikhael Bakhtin. *The Dialogic Imagination*. C. Emerson and M. Holquist, trans. (Austin: University of Texas Press, 1981): 348.

7. Alasdair MacIntyre, *After Virtue* (South Bend, Ind.: University of Notre Dame Press, 1981).

8. John Dewey, *Democracy and Education* (New York: Macmillan Publishing, 1916): 4.

Below I argue that parents, teachers, and schools transmit core values to their children and students in a myriad of creative ways and contexts, and that this traditional form of character education often "sticks to the bones" of our children and young people whereas more progressive strategies may miss the mark. More specifically, I consider two classical forms of a character education that require a process of moral transmission. First, I examine how parents and educators transmit values to their young by using and reinforcing a set of maxims and wise sayings that have motivational and moral significance. Second, I examine how educators transmit the values of honesty, trust, and integrity to older students through school-based honor codes. My purpose in examining these two traditional forms of moral education is to shed some light on their saliency and effectiveness in transmitting core values and ideals. I also explore how teaching maxims to children and implementing an honor code in high schools does or does not constitute a form of moral indoctrination. Finally, I anticipate and confront the question that I suspect concerns all progressive and character educators: Does transmitting moral maxims and the concept of honor to our young inhibit or impede their ability to develop their own sense of moral autonomy?

Maxims to Live By

For the past several years I have asked literally hundreds of people of all ages to share with me a maxim or "wise saying" that has been passed on to them. For example, my best friend told me that as he grew up his father said to him repeatedly "A job worth doing is a job worth doing well." To this day, my friend still hears the voice of his dad as he approaches an important project. Indeed, while I wrote this chapter my twelve-year-old son, Tyler, told me about a maxim that he learned while talking to his friend, Chris. They were discussing how hard it would be for anyone to break the school record for the mile run. Chris turned to Tyler and said, "Maybe so, but winners never quit, and quitters never win." Not surprisingly, Chris told Tyler that his soccer coach uses that saying all the time.

I define a maxim as a concise formulation of a fundamental principle or rule of conduct. Scholars have often commented that the appeal of these wise sayings owes much to their compact, memorable nature as well as to their usefulness and timelessness. Although some maxims contain a pronounced moral purpose ("You are only as good as your word"), other maxims clearly do not ("Absence makes the heart grow fonder"). My own research focuses on how parents, family members, and teachers transmit wise sayings to children that have (potentially at least) moral and motivational power.

Maxims constitute civilization's "memory bank." Humanity has preserved these wise sayings because they encapsulate a fundamental principle that transcends the conventions of a particular culture or society. The frozen word order and archaic lexicon of many maxims ("Do unto others as you would have them do unto you") also mark their timeliness and sense of moral authority, which extend beyond the speaker. Indeed, maxims uncover the voice of a second party—the commanding voice of one's elders, sages, or sacred ancestors. Consequently, whether maxims are seen as embodying universal truths or the norms of a society, they undeniably distill expressions of wisdom, or what Meider and colleagues call "apparent truths that have common currency" within a particular culture or society.[9]

Young people usually encounter a maxim by hearing it from another person—often a parent, relative, or teacher—within a specific social situation. In most cases, the person speaking or transmitting the maxim is attempting to exhort, persuade, inspire, offer caution, or to make a point. How many of us, during childhood, have heard our mothers say to us and our squawking siblings, "Two wrongs do not make a right"? As young people, we discovered the meaning of this exhortation

9. See S. Meider, S. A. Kingsbury, and K. B. Harder, *A Dictionary of American Proverbs* (New York: Oxford University Press, 1992).

by our mothers' repeated use of the maxim. It is very likely that our mothers neither intentionally explained the meaning of the maxim, nor told us how they learned it, nor why it was so meaningful to them. Although the use of the maxim occurred mostly within the context of sibling conflict ("He hit me first!"), we eventually extended the meaning and use of this particular maxim to situations that had nothing to do with sibling rivalry. Today, we may even use the maxim in exactly the same context as our mothers did, now with our own children and grandchildren.

A growing body of research indicates, interestingly, that some cultures emphasize the "proverb tradition" more than others. Strong evidence demonstrates that proverbs within the African-American culture have a long and distinguished history as important "cultural keepsakes." Rarely taught to children in any formal context, these nuggets of truth are commonly discovered by the young while interacting with family and elders. In Prhalad's splendid book, *African-American Proverbs in Context*, he recalls how he came to appreciate the power of this linguistic form:

> I fell in love with proverbs at an early age. I began collecting sayings from calendars and asking older people what they meant by some of the things that they said . . . [W]hen I was taken on walks through the woods and shown the beauty and mystery of plants, I might be told a proverb as a part of that experience. Or a story might be told about an enslaved ancestor who performed an incredible feat, with a proverb accompanying the narrative.[10]

Prhalad contends that adult-child interactions in general, and the in-home setting in particular, are the most fertile contexts for proverb and maxim use within the African-American community. Analyzing data from a number of sources, he concludes, "[W]hen informants are asked

10. Anand Prhalad, *African-American Proverbs in Context* (Jackson: University Press of Mississippi, 1996): 122.

where they learned the proverbs that they use, most of their examples involve a parent using the proverb to them."

Much of Prhalad's fieldwork focuses on individuals he calls "proverb masters." His research indicates that these individuals share several characteristics: (1) they usually grew up in a home where there was a "proverb master," often an older relative such as a grandmother, from whom they learned to interpret and apply proverbs; (2) they tend to have been and remain very emotionally connected with that person; and (3) they usually assume the position of bearer and active guardian of the African-American cultural tradition. Significantly, Prhalad posits that these men and women begin their "apprenticeship" early in life, imitating the proverbs of their parents and grandparents, and then sharing their wise sayings with other children on the playground.

Prhalad also documents how children often hear and learn particular maxims and wise sayings from their teachers. For example, Prhalad acquaints us with Mrs. Dorothy Bishop, who teaches at Golden Gate Elementary School in Oakland, California. During his fieldwork at the school, Prhalad was astonished at the number of times that Mrs. Bishop used different proverbs to motivate her students. In addition, anecdotal evidence indicates that teachers frequently use maxims in their classrooms as devices to inspire ("Nothing ventured, nothing gained"), to caution ("What goes around comes around"), or to redirect the behavior of their students ("If you cannot saying something nice, say nothing").

In his recent memoir *Teachers of My Youth*, the distinguished philosopher of education, Israel Scheffler, reflects on the value one of his teachers placed on reciting and memorizing particular biblical passages:

> In memorizing and reciting, we had used not only our eyes and ears but our vocal cords, not only our receptive apparatus but also our motor equipment—getting the feel of producing the words. [I]n becoming ours, these words would occasionally arise in our minds spontaneously; they would appear and sing freely, without waiting for an invitation. *They still visit me to this day and I am grateful to Mr.*

> *Leideker for having such a stress on what is now often scorned as an outmoded pedagogical procedure* (emphasis added).[11]

Clearly, reciting a maxim aloud repeatedly or writing it in a copybook are two time-honored memorization strategies used by generations of elders and teachers. Whether they are Prhalad's proverb masters or teachers such as Mr. Leideker, elders have historically borne the responsibility to transmit these words of wisdom to their young.

Let me state my point emphatically: *While teachers should strive to have their students invest personal meaning in a wise saying, relying solely on affective or associative attachment to a set of maxims or proverbs without memorization strategies is ill-advised and shortsighted.* Drill and practice are essential components of a successful performance, whether it is on the athletic field, in the concert hall, or in a civic-minded and ethical life. If isolated from other strategies that guide students to connect what they are memorizing to their own experiences, drill does kill. Memory research confirms that information is more quickly and firmly embedded in memory when it is tied to meaningful experience, emotion, and personal motivation. However, I suggest that character educators should employ in their schools and classrooms the traditional method of challenging their students to memorize maxims and to develop creative strategies that help their students connect a particular maxim to their own experiences, feelings, and motivations.

Let's assume a high school teacher wants her children to learn the Christopher Brothers-inspired proverb, "It is better to light a single candle than to curse the darkness." Utilizing a number of strategies, she might guide her students to connect the meaning of the proverb to their own ethical experiences and moral identities. When have they stood up to confront a wrong or an injustice instead of simply turning the other way? She might also explain why this proverb is important to her (perhaps why she is a member of Amnesty International), or she might

11. Israel Scheffler, *Teachers of My Youth: An American Jewish Experience* (Boston: Kluwer Academic Publishers, 1995): 98.

offer examples of historical and contemporary moral exemplars who have embodied the proverb (such as Aleksandr Solzhenitsyn or Mother Teresa). Finally, she should develop an assessment tool to determine whether her students have developed the ability to grasp the meaning and importance of the proverb. Her assessment, however, should also include whether her students have successfully memorized the proverb.

Why is memorization of a maxim an important teaching outcome? I think E. D. Hirsch and his colleagues had it just right when they argued that there exists a cluster of maxims and proverbs that "every American needs to know."[12] Just as stakeholders debated and eventually agreed on which core values should serve as guideposts for their character education programs, my own view is that local communities and educators should discern which maxims are most critical or important for children to learn.[13] The point I want to underscore is that educators and elders have a historical responsibility to intentionally transmit a set of cultural keepsakes to our young. Although approaches and curricula have changed dramatically, for several millennia elders have provided their young with an apprenticeship into responsible adulthood. The challenge for us today is to weave a character education that emphasizes personal meaning as well as the time-honored method of memorizing maxims that have moral and motivational power.

12. E. D. Hirsch, J. Kett, and J. Trefil, *The Dictionary of Cultural Literacy: What Every American Needs to Know* (New York: Dell Publishing, 1998).

13. With support from the John Templeton Foundation, a number of communities and schools have begun to help their students identify a set of core maxims. For example, under the leadership of Donald Biggs and Robert Colesante, high school and elementary students in Albany, New York, recently interviewed adults and mentors in Albany to learn which maxims and wise sayings are used in the African-American community to transmit the importance of working hard and setting goals. See Robert Colesante and Donald Biggs, *The Fifth Albany Institute for Urban Youth Leadership Development: Teaching and Advocating for the Work Ethic*. Final report to the John Templeton Foundation, 2000.

A Code of Honor to Live By

Considerable anecdotal evidence suggests that today educators are struggling to find effective ways to transmit and inculcate a set of core values beyond the elementary school years. Clearly, most character education programs that emphasize core values are designed for K-6 students. By the time students enter high school, what we commonly call character education has often been conflated or watered down to mean nothing more than the prevention of harmful behaviors: alcohol and drug prevention, violence prevention, pregnancy prevention. These prevention programs focus largely on what high school students should avoid and rarely (if at all) do these initiatives reinforce or emphasize the constellation of core values that served as ethical touchstones during the elementary school years. There are some glaring exceptions to this rule. In this chapter, I would like to focus on the few private high schools in the United States that have an honor code system that forms the moral center from which all other activities related to character education spiral out. Although none of these schools advertise or even suggest that their honor code serves as a panacea or prophylactic to the array of harmful behaviors highlighted above, they proudly defend their honor code system as one of the primary pedagogical vehicles by which school officials, older students, parents, and alumni transmit the institution's core values to new and returning students.

At the postsecondary level, and largely through the efforts of the Center for Academic Integrity, a growing number of colleges and universities are initiating campus-wide programs to identify a set of fundamental values that underpin the standards of academic integrity. These core values include honesty, trust, respect, fairness, and responsibility. Recently, the Center has disseminated data collected by Donald McCabe and his colleagues showing that college campuses with academic honor codes do indeed have lower levels of student dishonesty than schools with other sorts of initiatives designed to uphold the importance of academic integrity.[14] Taken together, the anecdotal and empirical evidence is compelling and clear: *honor codes are effective in transmitting a set of core values to students.* The question I explore below is *why*.

What is an honor code? In high school settings only, at the most simplistic level, a school's honor code is nothing but a cluster of words that explain a school's policy related to honest and dishonest conduct. In most schools this policy is limited to academic work, while some honor codes may extend to all domains of personal and social responsibility. Whether a high school student reads about the code in the school handbook, learns about it during the admission or orientation process, or hears about it from faculty or fellow students, for most new students the honor code is likely to represent (at least in the beginning) nothing more than an official injunction against lying, stealing, or cheating related to academic work. Most administrators and faculty involved in honor education agree that personal interactions and experiences with the concept of honor is almost always required before new students begin to feel a sense of personal ownership related to the school's honor code.

There are several discrete approaches by which an honor code system is transmitted to students. For example, on some campuses a school's honor code has a strong tradition or history, and this story is transmitted to new students in a wide variety of ways—from historical narratives in the student handbook and school website to personal narratives during convocation where an administrator, faculty member, current student, or recent alumnus exhorts the students to uphold the "[fill in school's name] honor system." Almost all schools (both secondary and postsecondary) hold a ceremony or honor convocation at the beginning of the academic year where the school formally asks each student to take an oath (either in writing or verbally) stating that he or

14. See Donald McCabe and Patrick Drinan, "Towards a Culture of Academic Integrity," *The Chronicle of Higher Education* (October 15, 1999): B7.

she will live by the fundamental values embodied in the honor system. When a strong honor system is in place, the honor code is reinforced and upheld by faculty members throughout the academic year.

Perhaps most important are the interactions of newer students with student leaders, who serve as the strongest defenders and advocates for the honor system. In many cases, these student leaders have the primary responsibility to educate the entire student body about the honor code system. Educators often remark that the depth of commitment that these students express and model in relation to the values of the honor code is critical in helping other students to understand that the honor system is not a cold structure but a "felt ideal." Perhaps the motto of the cadets who serve on the honor code committee at West Point says it all: "The more we educate, the less we investigate."

Finally, there are some students who come before the honor board or council itself, having been accused or found in violation of the honor system. In the publication *A Handbook for Developing and Sustaining Honor Codes* by David Gould (which focuses solely on honor systems at the high school level), a student from Saint Andrew's High School, Boca Raton, Florida, offers his own unique perspective on what is learned when a student appears before a school's honor council:

> The experience of being brought before the honor board is far more powerful than that of being brought before the dean of students, for example. Here, a student must not only face his or her bad decisions, but he or she must also do so in front of a panel of peers. Having never come before the Saint Andrew's honor board, I do not know the range of feelings that might surface during a hearing, but as a member of the honor board, *I can infer from students brought before the board that shame might be a predominant emotion.* A group of peers, some of whom might be in this student's classes, have said that what he or she did was wrong and his or her actions did not meet the expectations of the student body. The power of such an experience should not be underestimated. I have known or heard of several students who, as ninth or tenth graders, were brought before the honor board and who subsequently become so dedicated to honor that, as eleventh or twelfth

> graders, they were chosen by faculty and students to join the honor board (emphasis added).[15]

The student's use of the term "shame" is critical here. The concept of honor, and how the ideal of honor is transmitted, cannot be fully understood or operationalized unless we understand the relationship between honor and shame. Damon has written that shame is a moral emotion that can form and shape our hearts and minds.[16] This sort of shame is not toxic, certainly not in the way that shame is talked about most of the time in our contemporary culture. Instead, the avoidance of shame is often a powerful and positive moral motivator.[17]

The Greeks knew this well. *Aidos*, a term common to Greek plays and philosophy, denotes sensitivity to and protectiveness of one's self image. This moral emotion is not just a bodily sensation such as fear or anger; instead, *aidos* is an intense negative appraisal of the self. The moral emotion of *aidos* is felt when an individual believes he or she has committed a wrong.[18]

Within the context of classical Greek society, several components needed to be in place for a person to feel ashamed. First, there needs to be an audience. Unlike the feelings of guilt or embarrassment, feelings of honor and shame are inextricably bound up with a respected group of people. The etymology of the term "honor" clearly illustrates this reciprocal relationship. The term comes from the Latin *honos*, meaning an honor (such as receiving an honorary degree) awarded to

15. David Gould, *A Handbook for Developing and Sustaining Honor Codes* (Atlanta: Council for Spiritual and Ethical Education, 1999): 55.

16. William Damon, *The Moral Child* (New York: Free Press, 1988).

17. The concepts of honor and shame can only be understood within their historical context. In addition, honor and shame have historically meant something quite different for men and women. For a feminist analysis of shame, see Barbara Eurich-Roscoe and Hendrika Kemp, *Femininity and Shame: Women, Men, and Giving Voice to the Feminine* (New York: University Press of America, 1997).

18. I am indebted to Douglas Cairns's magisterial examination of the *aidos* concept. See Douglas Cairns, *Aidos: The Psychology and Ethics of Honour and Shame in Ancient Greek Literature* (Oxford: Clarendon Press, 1993).

someone. Thus, the concept of honor historically was not something you have, but something given to you (by those you respect and whose respect you seek). For example, in *Richard II* Shakespeare writes, "Mine honor is my life. Take honor from me and my life is done." At their fundamental core, the concepts of honor and shame are bound up with our obligations to others and our concern for the opinion of others.

Second, in Greek culture the emotion of shame emerges only when an individual has fallen short of a moral ideal that establishes what kind of person an individual is or would like to be. This is an important point to reinforce. Greek society placed great emphasis on the "excellences of persons" and on striving to attain such excellence in the right way, at the right time, for the right reasons. Thus, shame occurs only when an individual has strong desires to be a particular kind of person—and fails. Perhaps this may explain why a person of honor does what is right even in the absence of potential sanctions or the possibility of getting caught.[19]

Last, Greek society emphasized education as essential to honor. The elders knew that educating their young to have right desires was far more important than legislating laws and sanctions. For the Greeks (as well as for those in contemporary times), there are three time-tested methods used by educators to effectively transmit a moral standard of honor against which an individual or school wishes to be measured: (1) the ideal of honor needs to be clearly established, reinforced, and defended; (2) fundamental values of honor must be consistently modeled by teachers and elders; (3) ample opportunities for the young to practice (and eventually habituate) the values linked with the ideal of honor must be provided.

What is most important to recognize in terms of moral development theory is that a person's attachment to the ideal of honor is both a cognitive and affective achievement. Aristotle calls this state *hexeis*, a

19. This perspective is frequently advanced by scholars in response to Plato's question about the Ring of Gyges: Why would anyone not use the ring (which made the wearer invisible) to "take what he wanted from the market without fear?"

settled disposition that is long-lasting and therefore hard to change. That is, individuals who have internalized the virtues of honor (perhaps student leaders of the honor system) choose to uphold the honor code not because they fear being shamed or disgraced by their peers, but because they have acquired a personal, often emotional and visceral, revulsion against dishonest actions. This may help us better to understand the meaning of the phrase "for the love of honor." Even individuals who are less emotionally attached to the concept of honor have a set of sturdy cognitive hooks to grab. They may realize that they can never be proud of anything they got by cheating, or they may reason that cheating is unfair to all people, or perhaps they comprehend that a person who cheats in school now will find it easier to cheat in other situations later in life, perhaps even in one's closest personal relationships.[20]

I am aware that the portrait I have painted of Greek moral culture and the significance of honor and shame in that society is a historical ideal, and must be viewed against today's society, youth culture, and educational priorities. Indeed, there are real questions (even compelling statistics) about whether kids can "police" themselves in a contemporary culture where the dominant student code appears to be "thou shall not judge others." Data also suggest that students cheat to please their parents and to maintain (at all costs) a successful image. There is considerable data to suggest that teachers simply look the other way. All these factors challenge administrators, teachers, and students committed to implementing and sustaining an honor system at their schools.[21]

Let me emphasize that even when educators recognize that there has never been a honor system that works perfectly all the time (or always for the right reasons), instituting an honor code system in high

20. See Thomas Lickona, *Educating for Character: How Our Schools Can Teach Respect and Responsibility* (New York: Bantam Books, 1991): 77.

21. See Kevin Bushweller, "Generation of Cheaters," *The American School Board Journal* (April 1999): 24–32.

schools and colleges is anything but a form of indoctrination. An honor system impels, prompts, and motivates students to reflect on what it means to live in a community that affirms and defends a set of ideals related to honor and integrity. In this way, high schools that implement and reinforce an honor system are laboratories of moral learning, and student fidelity to the school's honor code is a powerful voice that counters society's prevailing perception that all of us are unencumbered, morally free agents. The moment students begin to care about upholding the honor system, they can no longer make whatever decisions they want. They cannot be moved by mere impulse or inclination. The fundamental values that constitute the ideal of honor not only limit their freedom but guide their moral actions. Establishing and sustaining an honor code system is a powerful way to transmit a set of values and ideals that extend beyond a shallow and brutish conception of ethical behavior summed up as, "You stay out of my business and I will stay out of yours."

Conclusion

This chapter had three objectives. First, I sought to examine how parents, teachers, and schools use maxims to transmit core values to young children and how honor codes transmit the values of honor to high-school students. Second, I wanted to explore whether these traditional character education approaches constituted a form of moral indoctrination. Last, I hoped to shed some light on whether the use of maxims and honor systems inhibits or impedes a young person's ability to develop his or her own moral autonomy.

We need only look at Nazi Germany or Mao's China to agree with progressive educators that indoctrination has reared its ugly head in the twentieth century. Specifically, scholars have determined that indoctrination occurs in schools and classrooms when: (1) the intention of a teacher or school is to make students believe in something despite the evidence; (2) the teaching methods are coercive or clearly inappropriate; (3) the content consists of prescribed doctrines and ideologies and everything else is strictly prohibited; and (4) the consequence of the education results in a closed, intolerant mind.[22]

My position is that the use of maxims and honor codes in our schools doesn't even come close to the threshold of indoctrination. I urge all progressive educators to stop using the term "indoctrination" when describing the objectives of character education. The term is an affront to the thousands of people—men and women, liberal and conservative, of all ethnicities and religions—who care deeply that American society, specifically our young people, may be experiencing moral vertigo. Instead, these educators should feel free to use the term "transmission." Character educators desperately want to transmit core values to our students. We are trying our best to pass on a substantial ethical endowment to our children. Even John Dewey emphasizes that this is the solemn responsibility of each generation. He writes:

> The things in civilization we most prize are not of ourselves. They exist by grace of the doings and sufferings of the continuous human community in which we are a link. *Ours is the responsibility of conserving, transmitting, rectifying and expanding the heritage of values* we have received that those who come after us may receive it more solid and secure, more widely accessible and more generously shared than we have received it (emphasis added).[23]

We must recognize, however, that there are real differences between progressive and character educators on what is meant by the term "moral autonomy." Among character educators, there is a prevailing sentiment that progressive educators want to encourage every young person to metaphorically climb his or her own Mt. Sinai and return with tablets on which he or she has written what is good and what is moral for him

22. I. A. Snook, *Indoctrination and Education* (London: Routledge & Kegan Paul, 1972).

23. John Dewey, *A Common Faith* (New Haven, Conn.: Yale University Press, 1934): 87.

or her alone. Moreover, the authors of these personalized tablets should feel free to amend them at any time, for any reason.

Progressive educators, on the other hand, perceive that character educators want to impose a moral education that begins and ends with the Ten Commandments. Here is the fundamental fault line today—a battle between David (the radically emancipated self) and Goliath (the wisdom of the past).

Where can we begin to bridge this gap? It might be helpful, in a spirit of humility, to initiate a dialogue that explores more deeply Dewey's call *to conserve, transmit, rectify and expand the heritage of values*. Many of us would agree that character educators seem to emphasize—both in rhetoric and practice—the strategies of conserving and transmitting, whereas progressive educators largely seek to rectify and expand our common constellation of values. Would it also be interesting to listen to character educators describe how they make sense of Dewey's call to expand and rectify our heritage of values, and learn the ways in which progressive educators do try to conserve and transmit values? How might a discussion on child development theories draw us closer to consensus on some of these essential questions? Would it be helpful to address the perception of progressive educators that character education seeks to emphasize a small cluster of core values such as obedience, punctuality, regularity, silence, and industry?[24] These are all critical questions.

Foremost, we should all strive to be more attentive to the terms we use to describe the moral development. For example, using the term

24. It is important to recognize that for over a century U.S. public schools have been influenced by a dominant perspective of schooling that has de-emphasized the moral functions of feeling and desire. This position was perhaps most forcefully delineated by William T. Harris, the first United States commissioner of education. In an influential 1888 report of the Committee in Moral Education of the National Council of Education he listed the virtues above as essential to the moral training of students. See John Elias, *Moral Education: Secular and Religious* (Malabar, Fla.: Robert E. Krieger Publishing Company, 1989): 24.

"integration" instead of "autonomy" or "internalization" might better enable us to understand that moral development includes integrating motivational and emotional systems with a set of moral values and ideals transmitted to us. "Integration" also suggests that this process of moral development is fragile, ongoing, and demands constant attention, instead of something that is sudden and dramatic (such as Paul's conversion experience on the road to Damascus). Moreover, the term suggests sensitivity to how unlikely it is that any of us are fully sovereign, radically autonomous moral beings. As Gus Blasi writes: "It is possible that the *integration* of moral understanding and motivation is not achieved at approximately the same age for the whole body of moral norms and virtues, but must be worked out separately for different issues" (emphasis added).[25] In other words, my best friend will always hear his father's voice telling him that "a job worth doing is a job worth doing well." Why is this voice any less *authentic* than his own?

There is also much work ahead for the field of character education. I agree with progressive educators that the language of moral energy and moral feeling, or what Carol Gilligan calls "felt knowledge," is too often absent from character education literature and programs.[26] Young people have a strong desire to know the world rather than simply get along with it. Our emotions are a critical component of the moral life, and without them our moral lives would be flat and empty. None of us are pure Kantians who live by duty alone. Emotions anchor our moral lives, and to sever this connection is to weaken the motivational springs of moral behavior. As I have said above, whether it is the use of maxims or upholding an honor code, our moral actions often flow from our attachment, commitment, and desire to a set of moral ideals. Character

25. Augusto Blasi, "Moral Understanding and Moral Personality: The Process of Moral Integration." In W. M. Kurtines and J. L. Lewirtz, eds., *Moral Development: An Introduction* (Boston: Allyn & Bacon, 1996): 238.

26. Carol Gilligan, "Adolescent Development Reconsidered," In *Approaches to Moral Education*, Andrew Garrod, ed. (New York: Teachers College Press, 1993): 104.

educators must find a way to more robustly integrate the fuel of emotion as a fundamental component of their programs and activities.

Here is where my own favorite maxim might help to bring these two educational perspectives together. The philosopher Charles Taylor once suggested that *strong convictions require strong sources*.[27] In other words, our convictions are forged within the crucible of personal experience and from the wisdom transmitted to us by family members, our religious tradition, our school traditions, and life lessons learned from a significant teacher or mentor. Unfortunately, these later sources of wisdom are too frequently neglected or overlooked, even in character education programs. Thus, the challenge for the next generation of character educators is to develop a pedagogy that inspires young people to integrate these sources of wisdom with their own moral experiences.

27. Charles Taylor, *Sources of the Self: The Making of Modern Identity* (Cambridge, Mass.: Harvard University Press, 1989).

How Moral Education Is Finding Its Way Back into America's Schools

Christina Hoff Sommers

Romanticism is always valuable as a protest. But another sort of trouble starts when romantics themselves get into positions of authority and demand that children shall scamper around being 'creative' and spontaneously 'discovering' what it has taken civilized man centuries to understand.[1]

—Professor Richard Peters
Philosopher of Education, Oxford

HANNAH ARENDT IS said to have remarked that every year civilization is invaded by the millions of tiny barbarians: they are called children. All cultures try to civilize the invaders by educating them and inculcating a sense of right and wrong. Ours, however, may be the first to question the propriety of doing so. What happens when democratic societies deprive children of the moral knowledge that took civilized

1. R. S. Peters, "Concrete Principles and Rational Passions." In *Moral Education: Five Lectures*, Nancy F. and Theodore R. Sizer, eds. (Cambridge, Mass.: Harvard University Press, 1970): 29.

man centuries to understand? What happens when educators celebrate children's creativity and innate goodness but abandon the ancestral responsibility to discipline, train, and civilize them? Unfortunately, we know the answer: we are just emerging from a thirty-year laissez-aller experiment in moral deregulation.

In the fall of 1996, I took part in a televised ethics program billed as a Socratic dialogue. For an hour, I joined another ethics professor, a history teacher, and seven high school students in a discussion of moral dilemmas. The program, "Ethical Choices: Individual Voices," was shown on public television and is now circulated to high schools for use in classroom discussions of right and wrong.[2] Its message still troubles me.

In one typical exchange, the moderator, Stanford law professor Kim Taylor-Thompson, posed this dilemma to the students. Your teacher has unexpectedly assigned you a five-page paper. You have only a few days to do it, and you are already overwhelmed with work. Would it be wrong to hand in someone else's paper? Two of the students found the suggestion unthinkable and spoke about responsibility, honor, and principle. "I wouldn't do it. It is a matter of integrity," said Elizabeth. "It's dishonest," said Erin. Two others saw nothing wrong with cheating. Eleventh-grader Joseph flatly said, "If you have the opportunity, you should use it." Eric concurred. "I would use the paper and offer it to my friends."

I have taught moral philosophy to college freshmen for more than fifteen years, so I was not surprised to find students on the PBS program defending cheating. There are some in every class, playing devil's advocate with an open admiration for the devil's position. That evening, in our PBS Socratic dialogue, I expected at least to have a professional ally in the other philosophy teacher, who surely would join me in making the case for honesty. Instead, the professor defected. He told the students that in this situation, it was the teacher who was immoral

2. "Ethical Choices: Individual Voices" (New York: Thirteen/WNET, 1997).

for having given the students such a burdensome assignment and was disappointed in us for not seeing it his way. "What disturbs me," he said, "is how accepting you all seem to be of this assignment . . . to me it's outrageous from the point of view of learning to force you to write a paper in this short a time."

Through most of the session the professor focused on the hypocrisy of parents, teachers, and corporations, but had little to say about the moral obligations of the students. When we discussed the immorality of shoplifting, he implied that stores are in the wrong for their pricing policies and he talked about "corporations deciding on a twelve percent profit margin . . . and perhaps sweatshops." The professor was friendly and, to all appearances, well-meaning. Perhaps his goal was to empower students to question authority and rules. That, however, is something contemporary adolescents already know how to do. Too often, we teach students to question principles before they even vaguely understand them. In this case, the professor advised high school students to question moral teachings and rules of behavior that are critical to their well-being.

The professor's hands-off style has been fashionable in the public schools for thirty years. It has gone under various names such as values clarification, situation ethics, and self-esteem guidance. These so-called value-free approaches to ethics have flourished at a time when many parents fail to give children basic guidance in right and wrong. The story of why so many children are being deprived of elementary moral training encompasses three or four decades of misguided reforms by educators, parents, and judges has yet to be entirely told. Reduced to its philosophical essentials, it is the story of the triumph of Jean-Jacques Rousseau over Aristotle.

Aristotle vs. Rousseau

Some 2,300 years ago Aristotle laid down what children need: clear guidance on how to be moral human beings. What Aristotle advocates became the default model for moral education over the centuries. He shows parents and teachers how to civilize the invading hordes of child barbarians. It is only recently that many educators have begun to denigrate his teachings. Aristotle regards children as wayward, uncivilized, and very much in need of discipline. The early Christian philosopher, St. Augustine, went further, regarding the child's refractory nature as a manifestation of the original sin committed by Adam and Eve when they rebelled against the dictates of God. Each philosopher, in his way, regards perversity as a universal feature of human nature. Aristotle compares moral education to physical training. Just as we become strong and skillful by doing things that require strength and skill, so, he says, do we become good by practicing goodness. Ethical education, as he understands it, is training in emotional control and disciplined behavior. Habituation to right behavior comes before an appreciation or understanding of why we should be good. He advocated first socializing children by inculcating habits of decency, using suitable punishments and rewards to discipline them to behave well. Eventually they understand the reasons and advantages of being moral human beings.

Far from giving priority to the free expression of emotion, Aristotle (and Plato) teaches that moral development is achieved by educating children to modulate their emotions. For Aristotle, self-awareness means being aware of and avoiding behaviors that reason proscribes but emotion dictates. "We must notice the errors into which we ourselves are liable to fall (because we all have different tendencies) . . . and then we must drag ourselves in the contrary direction."[3] Children with good moral habits gain control over the intemperate side of their natures and grow into free and flourishing human beings.

> The moral virtues . . . are engendered in us neither by nor contrary to nature; we are constituted by nature to receive them, but their full development is due to habit. . . . So it is a matter of no little importance

3. Aristotle, *Ethics*, trans. J.A.K. Thomson (London: Penguin, 1976): 109.

> what sort of habits we form from the earliest age—it makes a vast difference, or rather all the difference in the world.[4]

Aristotle's general principles for raising moral children were unquestioned through most of Western history; even today his teachings represent common-sense opinion about child rearing, but in the eighteenth century, the Aristotle's wisdom was directly challenged by the theories of the enlightenment philosopher Jean Jacques Rousseau. Rousseau denies that children are born wayward (originally sinful), insisting instead that children are, by nature, noble, virtuous beings who are corrupted by an intrusive socialization. The untutored child is spontaneously good and graceful. "When I picture to myself a boy of ten or twelve, healthy, strong and well-built for his age, only pleasant thoughts arise . . . . I see him bright, eager, vigorous, care-free, completely absorbed in the present, rejoicing in abounding vitality."[5]

According to Rousseau "the first education should be purely negative. . . . It consists not in teaching virtue or truth, but in preserving the heart from vice and the mind from error."[6] He rejects the traditional notion that moral education in the early stages must habituate the child to virtuous behavior:

> The only habit a child should be allowed to acquire is to contract none. . . . Prepare in good time for the reign of freedom and the exercise of his powers, but allowing his body its natural habits and accustoming him always to be his own master and follow the dictates of his will as soon as he has a will of his own.[7]

4. ——. *Ethics*: 92.

5. From Steven Cahn, ed. "Emile." In *The Philosophical Foundations of Education* (New York: Harper & Row, 1970): 163. Selection from *The 'Emile' of Jean-Jacques Rousseau: Selections*, William Boyd, ed. (New York: Teachers College, Columbia University, 1962): 11–128.

6. William Boyd, ed. *The 'Emile' of Jean-Jacques Rousseau*. (New York: Teachers College Press, 1970): 41.

7. Steven Cahn, *The Philosophical Foundations of Education*: 158.

Contrary to the received view, Rousseau believes the child's nature is originally good and free of sin. As he sees it, a proper education provides the soil for the flourishing of the child's inherently good nature, bringing it forth unspoiled and fully effective. In his view, the goal of moral education is defeated when an external code is imposed on children. Rousseau is modern in his distrust of socially ordained morals as well as in his belief that the best education elicits the child's own authentic (benevolent) nature. Rousseau emphatically rejects the Christian doctrine that human beings are innately rebellious and naturally sinful:

> Let us lay it down as an incontestable principle that the first impulses of nature are always right. There is no original perversity in the human heart.[8]

Although Rousseau is against instilling moral habits in a free and noble being, he allows that the child's development requires guidance and encouragement to elicit its own good nature. He urges parents and tutors to put the child's "kindly feelings into action."[9]

Christian and classical pagan thinkers are convinced that far more is needed. They insist that virtue cannot be attained without a directive moral training that habituates the child to virtuous behavior. Saint Augustine and the orthodox Christian thinkers are especially pessimistic about the efficacy of putting kindly feelings into action. According to Augustine, not even the most disciplined moral education guarantees a virtuous child: education without divine help (grace) is insufficient. By contrast, not only do Rousseau's followers deny the Augustinian doctrine that our natures are originally sinful and rebellious—they further regard directive moral education as an assault on the child's right to develop freely.

There is much to admire in Rousseau. He argued for humane child

8. Ibid., 162.
9. Ibid., 174.

rearing at a time when cruel rigidity was the norm. Though his criticisms of the educational practices of his day are valid, his own recommendations have simply not proved workable. It is, perhaps, worth noting that he did not apply his fine theories to his own life and was altogether irresponsible in dealing with his own children.[10] His theories, too, are marred by inconsistencies. On the one hand, he is firmly against instilling habits in a child; on the other, he dispenses a lot of sound Aristotelian advice to parents for habituating their children to the classical virtues: "Keep your pupil occupied with all the good deeds."

Despite his celebration of freedom, even Rousseau would be appalled by the permissiveness we see so much of today. "The surest way to make your child unhappy," he wrote, "is to accustom him to get everything he wants."[11] All the same, Rousseau parted company with the traditionalists on the crucial question of human nature. For better or worse, Rousseau's followers ignored his Aristotelian side and developed the progressive elements of his educational philosophy.

Though we wish to believe him, Rousseau's rosy picture of the child fails to convince. In *Emile*, Rousseau states that although children may do bad deeds, a child can never be said to be bad "because wrong action depends on harmful intention and that he will never have."[12] This flies in the face of common experience. Most parents and teachers will tell you that children often have harmful intentions. In perhaps the most famous description of children's "harmful intentions," Saint Augustine, in his *Confessions*, describes his boyhood pleasure in doing wrong—simply for the joy of flouting prohibitions. Some parents and teachers might indeed find Augustine's description of children's unruly nature understated and some will find Golding's *Lord of the Flies* an even more

10. He is said to have fathered five illegitimate children by an uneducated servant girl, Térese Le Vasseur. All the children were sent to foundling homes, which was the equivalent of a death sentence. See Ronald Grimsley, "Jean-Jacques Rousseau," in *Encyclopedia of Philosophy*, vol. 7 (New York: Macmillan, 1967): 218.

11. Cahn, *The Philosophical Foundations of Education*: 160.

12. Ibid., 163.

telling description of what children are naturally like than that of Augustine's wayward boyhood friends.

Rousseau powerfully dominates the thinking of the theorists whose influence pervades modern schools of education. In pedagogy, Rousseau's views inspired the progressive movement in education, which turned away from rote teaching and sought methods to free the child's creativity. Rousseau's ideas are also deployed to discredit the traditional directive style of moral education associated with Aristotelian ethical theory and Judeo-Christian religion and practice.

Value-Free Kids

The directive style of education, denigrated as indoctrination, was cast aside in the second half of the twentieth century and discontinued as the progressive style became dominant. By the seventies, character education had been effectively discredited and virtually abandoned in practice.

In 1970, Theodore Sizer, then dean of the Harvard School of Education, coedited with his wife, Nancy, a collection of ethics lectures entitled *Moral Education*.[13] The preface set the tone by condemning the morality of the Christian gentleman, the American prairie, the *McGuffey Readers*, and the hypocrisy of teachers who tolerate a grading system that is the "terror of the young."[14] The Sizers were especially critical of the "crude and philosophically simpleminded sermonizing tradition" of the nineteenth century. They referred to directive ethics education in all its guises as the old morality. According to the Sizers, leading moralists agree that that kind of morality "can and should be scrapped." The Sizers favored a new morality that gives primacy to students' autonomy and independence. Teachers should never preach or attempt to inculcate virtue; rather, through their actions, they should

13. Nancy F. and Theodore R. Sizer, eds. *Moral Education: Five Lectures.*
14. Ibid., 3–5.

demonstrate a fierce commitment to social justice. In part, that means democratizing the classroom: "Teacher and children can learn about morality from each other."[15]

The Sizers preached a doctrine already practiced in many schools throughout the country. Schools were scrapping the old morality in favor of alternatives that gave primacy to the children's moral autonomy. Values clarification was popular in the seventies and its proponents consider it inappropriate for a teacher to encourage students, however indirectly, to adopt the values of the teacher or the community. The cardinal sin is to impose values on the student. Instead, the teacher's job is to help the students discover their own values. In *Readings in Values Clarification*, two of the leaders of the movement, Sidney Simon and Howard Kirschenbaum, explain what is wrong with traditional ethics education:

> We call this approach "moralizing," although it has also been known as inculcation, imposition, indoctrination, and in its most extreme form, "brainwashing."[16]

Lawrence Kohlberg, a Harvard moral psychologist, developed cognitive moral development, a second favored approach. Kohlberg shared the Sizers' low opinion of traditional morality, referring disdainfully to the "old bags of virtues" that earlier educators had sought to inculcate.[17] Kohlbergian teachers were more traditional than the proponents of values clarification. They sought to promote a Kantian awareness of duty and responsibility in students. Kohlberg was traditional in his opposition to the moral relativism that many progressive educators found congenial; all the same, Kohlbergians shared with other progressives a scorn for any form of top-down inculcation of moral principles.

15. Ibid., 4.

16. Sidney Simon and Howard Kirschenbaum, *Readings in Values Clarification* (Minneapolis, Minn.: Winston Press, 1973): 18.

17. See, for example, Lawrence Kohlberg, "The Cognitive-Developmental Approach," *Phi Delta Kappan* (June 1975): 670–75.

They too believed in student-centered teaching, where the teacher acts less as a guide than as a facilitator of the student's development.

Kohlberg himself later changed his mind and conceded that his rejection of indoctrinative moral education had been a mistake.[18] His admirable recantation had little effect. The next fashion in progressive pedagogy, student-centered learning, was soon to leave the Kohlbergians and the values clarifiers far behind. By the late eighties, self-esteem education had become all the rage. Ethics was superseded by attention to the child's personal sense of well-being: the school's primary aim was to teach children to prize their rights and self-worth. In the old days, teachers asked seventh graders to write about "The Person I Admire Most." But in today's child-centered curriculum, they ask children to write essays celebrating themselves. In one popular middle school English text, an assignment called "The Nobel Prize for Being You" informs students that they are "wonderful" and "amazing" and instructs them to:

> Create two documents in connection with your Nobel Prize. Let the first document be a nomination letter written by the person who knows you best. Let the second be the script for your acceptance speech, which you will give at the annual award ceremony in Stockholm, Sweden.[19]

18. See Lawrence Kohlberg, "Moral Education Reappraised," *The Humanist* (November/December 1978): 14–15. Kohlberg, renouncing his earlier position, said:

Some years of active involvement with the practice of moral education . . . has led me to realize that my notion . . . was mistaken . . . The educator must be a socializer, teaching value content and behavior and not [merely] . . . a process-facilitator of development . . . I no longer hold these negative views of indoctrinative moral education and I [now] believe that the concepts guiding moral education must be partly 'indoctrinative.' This is true, by necessity, in a world in which children engage in stealing, cheating and aggression."

19. *Write Source 2000 Sourcebook* (Wilmington, Mass.: Houghton Mifflin, 1995): 217.

For extra credit, students can award themselves a trophy "that is especially designed for you and no one else."

Through most of human history, children learned about virtue and honor by hearing or reading the inspiring stories of great men and women. By the 1990s, this practice, which many educators regarded as too directive, was giving way to practices that suggested to students that they were their own best guides in life. This turn to the autonomous subject as the ultimate moral authority is a notable consequence of the triumph of the progressive style over traditional directive methods of education.

It's hard to see how the Harvard theorists who urged teachers to jettison the "crude and philosophically simpleminded sermonizing tradition of the nineteenth century" could defend the crude egoism that has replaced it. Apart from the philosophical niceties, there are concrete behavioral consequences. The moral deregulation that the New England educators required took hold in the very decades that saw a rise in conduct disorders among children in the nation's schools. No doubt much, perhaps most, of this trend can be ascribed to the large social changes that weakened family and community, but some of the blame can be laid at the doors of all the well-intentioned professors who helped undermine the schools' traditional mission of morally edifying their pupils.

Few thinkers have written about individual autonomy with greater passion and good sense than the nineteenth-century philosopher John Stuart Mill. Mill clearly is talking about adults. "We are not speaking of children," he says in *On Liberty*.[20] "Nobody denies that people should be so taught and trained in youth as to know and benefit by the ascertained results of human experience." Mill could not foresee the advent of thinkers like the Sizers and the values clarificationists who glibly recommended scrapping the old morality.

20. John Stuart Mill, *On Liberty* (Chicago: Regnery Press, 1955): 14.

Where the Reformers Go Wrong

Progressive educators who follow Rousseau are at pains to preserve the child's autonomy. They frown on old-fashioned moralizing, preaching, and threats of punishment, regard such methods as coercive, and believe instead that children should discover for themselves, by their own rational faculties, which actions are moral. This laissez-aller policy abandons children to their fate. The purpose of moral education is not to preserve our children's autonomy, but to develop the character they will rely on as adults. As Aristotle persuasively argues, children who have been helped to develop good moral habits will find it easier to become autonomous adults. Conversely, children who have been left to their own devices will founder.

Those who oppose directive moral education often call it a form of brainwashing or indoctrination. That is sheer confusion. When you brainwash people, you undermine their autonomy, their rational self-mastery. You diminish their freedom. But when you educate children to be competent, self-controlled and morally responsible, you increase their freedom and enlarge their humanity. The Greeks and Romans understood this very well. So did the great scholastic and enlightenment thinkers. Indeed, a first principle of every great religion and high civilization is to know what is right and act on it. This is the highest expression of freedom and personal autonomy. To suggest that we place more emphasis on instilling a sense of responsibility and civility than on alerting children to their civil and personal rights under law may sound quaint, quixotic, or even reactionary but is practical and achievable. Despite appearances to the contrary, most children respect civility and good manners. If their own manners are wanting, it is because so little is expected of them.

Common sense, convention, tradition, and even modern social science[21] research all converge in support of the Aristotelian tradition

21. See, for example, Laurence Steinberg in *Beyond the Classroom: Why School*

of directive character education. Children need standards, they need clear guidelines, they need adults in their lives who are understanding but firmly insistent on responsible behavior, but a resolute adherence to standards has been out of fashion in education circles for more than thirty years. An Aristotelian education is still the child's best bet. Unfortunately, our era has been characterized by the ascendancy of Rousseau and a decided antipathy toward the directive inculcation of the virtues.

Two Badly Socialized Boys

In April 1999, the massacre at Columbine High School shocked an uncomprehending nation by its cold brutality. It was the seventh school shooting in less than two years. This time, more than ever, the public's need to make sense of such tragedies was palpable. How could it happen? The usual explanations made little sense. Poverty? Eric Harris and Dylan Klebold were not poor. Easy access to weapons? True, but young men, especially in the West, have always had access to guns. Divorce? Both boys' families were intact. A nation of emotionally repressed boys? Boys were much the same back in the fifties and sixties when nobody shot up schoolmates. And why American boys?

Asking, Why now? and, Why here? puts us on the track of what is missing in the American way of socializing children that was present in the recent past. To find answers, we need to attend to the views of the progressive-education theorists who advocated abandoning the traditional mission of indoctrinating children in the "old morality" and persuaded the American educational establishment to adopt instead the romantic moral pedagogy of Rousseau. Teachers and parents who embraced this view badly underestimated the potential barbarism of children who are not given a directive moral education. It is not likely that

---

Reform Has Failed and What Parents Need to Do (New York: Simon & Schuster, 1996).

a single ethics course would have been enough to stop boys like Harris and Klebold from murdering classmates. On the other hand, a K-12 curriculum infused with moral content might have created a climate that would make a massacre unthinkable. For such a depraved and immoral act was indeed unthinkable in the simpleminded days before the schools cast aside their mission of moral edification. An insistence on character education might have diminished the derisive mistreatment at the hands of more popular students suffered by the perpetrators, which apparently was one incitement for their gruesome actions.

Teachers, too, would have acted differently. Had K-12 teachers in the Littleton schools seen it as their routine duty to civilize the students in their care, they would never have overlooked the bizarre, antisocial behavior of Klebold and Harris. When the boys appeared in school with T-shirts with the words "Serial Killer" emblazoned on them, their teachers would have sent them home, nor would the boys have been allowed to wear swastikas or to produce grotesquely violent videos. By tolerating these modes of self-expression, the adults at Columbine High School implicitly sent the message to the students that there's not much wrong with the serial or mass murder of innocent people.

One English teacher at Columbine told *Education Week* that both boys had written short stories about death and killing "that were horribly, graphically, violent" and that she had notified school officials. According to the teacher, they took no action because nothing the boys wrote violated school policy. Speaking with painful irony, the frustrated teacher explained, "In a free society, you can't take action until they've committed some horrific crime because they are guaranteed freedom of speech."[22] In many high schools, students are confident that their right to free expression will be protected. Counselors and administrators, fearful of challenges by litigious parents who would be backed by the ACLU and other zealous guardians of students' rights, rarely take action.

22. *Education Week* (April 28, 1999): 16; see also *Education Week* (May 26, 1999): 14.

The love affair with Rousseau's romantic idealization of the child of American education has made it inevitable that our public schools fail to do their part in civilizing young "barbarians." Many schools no longer see themselves having a primary role in moral edification. The style is not to interfere with the child's self-expression and autonomy. Leaving children to discover their own values is a little like putting them in a chemistry lab full of volatile substances and saying, "Discover your own compounds, kids." We should not be surprised when some blow themselves up and destroy those around them.

A Wind of Change

Even before the spate of school shootings raised public concern about the moral climate in the nation's schools, voices called for reform. In the early nineties, a hitherto silent majority of parents, teachers, and community leaders began to agitate in favor of old-fashioned moral education. In July 1992, one group called the Character Counts Coalition (organized by the Josephson Institute of Ethics and made up of teachers, youth leaders, politicians, and ethicists) gathered in Aspen, Colorado, for a three-and-a-half-day conference on character education. At the end of the conference, the group put forward the Aspen Declaration on Character Education.[23] Among its principles:

- The present and future well-being of our society requires an involved, caring citizenry with good moral character.
- Effective character education is based on core ethical values which form the foundation of democratic society—in particular, respect, responsibility, trustworthiness, caring, justice, fairness, civic virtue, and citizenship.

23. "Aspen Declaration on Character Education," available through the Josephson Institute, Marina Del Ray, California; or Kevin Ryan, Director, Boston University Center for the Advancement of Ethics and Character.

- Character education is, first and foremost, an obligation of families. It is also an important obligation of faith communities, schools, youth and other human service organizations.

The Character Counts Coalition has attracted a wide and politically diverse following. Its board of advisers includes liberals such as Marian Wright Edelman and conservatives such as William Bennett. Ten United States senators from both political parties have joined, along with a number of governors, mayors, and state representatives. The new character education movement is gaining impetus.

Today, schools throughout the country are finding their way back to contemporary versions of directive moral education. Teachers, administrators, and parents are again getting into the business of making it clear to students that they must behave honorably, courteously, and kindly, that they must work hard and strive for excellence. Several state departments of education and numerous large-city boards of education, including those of St. Louis, Chicago, Hartford, and San Antonio, have mandated an ethics curriculum. In some schools the whole curriculum is shaped by these imperatives.

Fallon Park Elementary School in Roanoke, Virginia, for example, has seen a dramatic change in its students since the principal adopted the Character Counts program in 1998.[24] Every morning the students recite the Pledge of Allegiance. This is followed by a pledge written by the students and teachers: "Each day in our words and actions we will persevere to exhibit respect, caring, fairness, trustworthiness, responsibility and citizenship. These qualities will help us to be successful students who work and play well together." According to the principal, suspensions have declined sixty percent, attendance and grades have improved, and—*mirabile dictu*—misbehavior on the bus has all but disappeared. The school's gym instructor, who has been there for twenty-nine years, has noticed a change. The kids are practicing good

24. See *Washington Post* (February 4, 1999): metro, 1.

sportsmanship, and even school troublemakers seem to be changing for the better. She recently noticed one such boy encouraging a shy girl to join a game. "It almost brought tears to my eyes . . . this is the best year ever in this school."

Vera White, principal of Jefferson Junior High in Washington, D.C., was stunned some years ago to realize that children from her school had been part of an angry mob that attacked police and firefighters with rocks and bottles. "Those are my children. If they didn't care enough to respect the mayor and the fire marshal and everyone else, what good does an education do?" She decided to make character education central to the mission of her school. Students now attend assemblies that focus on positive traits such as respect and responsibility. Ms. White initiated the program in 1992; since then theft and fighting have been rare. Unlike other schools in the area, Jefferson has no bars on the windows and no metal detectors.[25]

William F. Washington Jarvis, headmaster at the Roxbury Latin School in Boston and an Episcopal priest, has always emphasized character and discipline, but others are now joining him. Jarvis holds a harsh, non-Rousseauian view of human nature: left untrained, we are "brutish, selfish, and capable of great cruelty. We must do our utmost to be decent and responsible, and we must demand this of our children and our students." Whenever they behave badly, says the headmaster, "We have to hold up a mirror to the students and say, 'This is who you are. Stop it.'"[26]

Contrast these schools with a school like Columbine High. We know that the Littleton killers had attended anger-management seminars, met weekly with a "diversion" officer, attended a Mothers Against Drunk Driving panel, and did compulsory community service. But it seems they never encountered a Reverend Jarvis or a Principal White.

25. *Dallas Morning News* (March 10, 1995): 1C.

26. Wray Herbert and Missy Daniel, "The Moral Child," *U.S. News & World Report* (June 3, 1996): 52.

After Littleton, many a barn door is being shut and padlocked, but a spokesperson for the Littleton school district had it right when she asked, "Do you make a high school into an armed prison camp where there are metal detectors that make kids feel imprisoned, or do you count on people's basic goodness and put good rules in place?"[27]

One very promising program for putting good rules in place is the Youth Charter, developed by William Damon, a professor of education at Stanford University and a leading authority on moral education.[28] Damon's program calls for communities to work out a code of conduct for children. Youth Charter helps parents and schools set rules and standards that make clear to children what is expected of them.

Although the movement to reinstate directive moral education is gathering momentum, it is being fiercely resisted in some quarters by those who find it educationally retrograde. Amherst professor Benjamin DeMott wrote a scathing piece for *Harper's* magazine a few years ago jeering at the reviving character education movement. He asked how we can hope to teach ethics in a society where CEOs award themselves large salaries in the midst of downsizing. Thomas Lasley, Dean of the University of Dayton School of Education, denounces what he calls the values juggernaut. Alfie Kohn, a noted education speaker and writer, accuses schools that are active in character education of indoctrinating children and blighting them politically. "Children in American schools are even expected to begin each day by reciting a loyalty oath to the Fatherland, although we call it by a different name."[29] Kohn's comparison—likening the Pledge of Allegiance to a loyalty oath in Hitler's Reich—is a fair example of the mindset one still finds among some progressives.

Will the educational philosophy of the Kohns, Lasleys, De Motts,

27. *Education Week* (April 28, 1999): 17.

28. William Damon, *The Youth Charter: How Communities Can Work Together to Raise Standards for All Our Children* (New York: Free Press, 1997).

29. Alfie Kohn, "How Not to Teach Values: A Critical Look at Character Education," *Phi Delta Kappan* (February 1997): 433.

and Sizers prevail? The answer is "no, not any longer." It appears that parents, teachers, school administrators, and community leaders have finally been alerted and alarmed, and are beginning to assert their wills. Programs like Character Counts and the Youth Charter are flourishing and new programs are starting up all the time. Nan Dearen, executive director of Kids with Character in Dallas, has characterized this momentum: "They say character education is a grassroots movement, but it just spreads like wildfire."[30] Kevin Ryan, director of the Center for the Advancement of Ethics and Character at Boston University, expresses the movement's confidence and resolve: "Society will not put up with value-neutral education."[31]

* * *

Social critics often refer to the Law of Unintended Consequences. According to this law, seemingly benign social or political changes often have unfortunate, even disastrous, side effects. Few romantic idealists of the 1920s and 1930s, for example, had any idea that applying utopian principles to real societies might cause their total degradation. Nor did anyone in the 1970s expect that applying Rousseau's perspective to moral education would set children adrift, denying to them the essential guidance they need in life. Fortunately, a Law of Fortuitous Reversals also operates in social life. According to this second law, when bad, unintended consequences seem irreparable, the situation suddenly improves dramatically. One fortuitous reversal was the rapid, unforeseen disintegration of the Soviet system a decade ago. Another, just under way, is the unexpected return of Aristotelian common sense in the moral education of American children.

30. Colleen O'Connor, "The We Decade: Rebirth of Community," *The Dallas Morning News* (March 10, 1995): 1.

31. Scott Baldauf, "Reading, Writing, and Right and Wrong," *The Christian Science Monitor* (August 27, 1996): 1.

The Science of Character Education

Marvin W. Berkowitz

THE FIELD OF character education is rife with controversy as debates question whether the focus should be on virtues, values, behaviors, or reasoning capacities. Controversy swirls around the varied approaches to implementing character education: experiential learning, peer debate, indoctrinative teaching, community service, participatory governance, reading about character, and so on. Many of these debates have strong roots in theoretical and philosophical differences.

However, when and if the dust settles, it should be clear that the bottom line of character education is not philosophical distinctions, pedagogical ideologies, politics, or other conceptual disagreements. Rather, it is the development of children. In this chapter, I will attempt to take a very focused and practical approach to character education, to take a stab at beginning what can become a science of character education. I will examine what we mean by character, how it develops, and what can be done to foster its optimal development.

This work was supported by a grant from the John Templeton Foundation.

A Word about Words

Before we can explore what we know (and don't know) about character development and character education, we need to discuss terminology. The labels for this field vary by history, geography, and ideology. Currently in the United States, the term du jour is character education. That is the term I have chosen to use in this chapter. However, only a decade or two ago, the more popular term was moral education. The term moral still tends to be preferred in many other countries, especially in Asia, although one group in Japan has wedded the term to psychology and produced a new term, "moralogy." Preceding that, values education was in vogue in the United States. Values education is, in fact, the currently preferred term in Great Britain (although the Scottish Consultative Council on the Curriculum prefers the term values in education whereas others in Great Britain prefer values education). Furthermore, different theoretical perspectives are aligned more with one or another of these various terms. In the United States, character education has been aligned most closely with more conservative, traditional, and behavioral approaches. Moral education has been aligned with more liberal, constructivist, and cognitive approaches. Values education has been aligned with more atheoretical, attitudinal, empirical approaches. At this point in the discussion, I expect you to be quite confused and even annoyed at this degree of terminological disagreement. I know I am. Do not panic, however, because I will, from here on use the terms character development and character education to represent all these disparate points of view, and you can now proceed to forget the confusion that I have just outlined for you.

There has been too much of the "my theory can beat up your theory" mentality in the field. I prefer a more dialectical approach, whereby the intersections and conflicts between different approaches can be used to generate agreements, compromises, and best solutions. It is time to use science to help kids become good people rather than lay out landmines of theory disagreements.

This diversity and disagreement have led to a rather fractionated perspective on what I refer to as character development. In this chapter, I choose to use the term character (only in part because I hold the title of Sanford N. McDonnell Professor of Character Education); however, I use it as an integrative, bridging term. One goal of this chapter is to build bridges across the theoretical chasms that have been dug by contentious warring factions in this field. Actually, I am rather uninterested in terminology. I would be just as happy to call the field moral education, which I did for over two decades, or to create a new all-encompassing rubric such as developmental education. In fact, I wouldn't mind calling it Henrietta or Blog or 2C3a#*11.a as long as it is defined clearly and as long as it optimally serves the development of socio-moral competency in children. As I said before, this is all about kids, not esoteric distinctions, labels, or factions. Those rarely serve kids' best interests.

Character Education: The State of the Art

Just as it is difficult to define character and find consensual labels for character education, it is difficult to summarize what contemporary character education entails. The term character education has come to encompass what used to be rather different fields. I will therefore try to provide a quick and dirty bird's-eye view of character education. Ideally, as we shall see later in this chapter, quality character education should be intentional and comprehensive—sometimes it is intentional; rarely is it comprehensive. The Character Education Partnership articulates standards for quality character education in their "Eleven Principles of Effective Character Education" and the corresponding "Character Education Quality Standards" (both of which can be accessed through their website: www.character.org). These standards include an explicit values agenda, schoolwide implementation, promoting positive relationships and intrinsic motivation, defining character comprehensively, partnering with parents and community, and being data-driven. It is rare to find schools or districts that fulfill all of these standards.

Most character education initiatives center around a set of words or concepts that represent the ethical agenda of the school; i.e., "words of the month" (or week, or even day) that identify the character outcomes identified as central to the school's mission by the school, community, or both. Those words sometimes are chosen by the school staff, sometimes by district staff or a community panel, and sometimes adopted from another source (such as the Character Counts's "six pillars of character"). What schools do with these words is quite variable. Although sometimes they simply pay lip-service to them, usually they display them prominently (on calendars, stationery, walls, and so on). They may use them as the foci for curriculum or extracurricular programming.

Often character education stands alone. Frequently middle schools and high schools put character education into homeroom or advisory class meetings or make it an elective or required class. Character education is typically part of the curriculum in literature and social studies classes, but it actually can appear in almost any part of the curriculum, including math and physical education. Many schools connect their character agenda with their service opportunities. Although service learning is a common vehicle for character education, any form of service may support character education.

Character education can focus on specific issues such as sex education, health education, environmental studies, multicultural education, peer conflict resolution, risk prevention, and religious studies. It may focus on fostering specific character outcomes such as moral reasoning (typically through ethical dilemma discussion) or altruism (through service).

Character education is less frequently manifested as comprehensive school reform. Models such as the Just Community School, Child Development Project, Responsive Classroom, and Resolving Conflict Creatively Program are all approaches that stress pervasive schoolwide culture transformation. Whereas all of these and other approaches are observed in schools, the justification for selecting one approach over another is often less than scientific. Typically it is based on convenience, external advocacy, limited knowledge, intuition, and so on. The bottom line is that what stands as character education is highly variable and infrequently meets the standards for quality. To create a true science of character education, we need to back up and explore what we mean by character, how it develops, and what we know about how schools can effectively foster its development.

What Is Character?

It is impossible to foster optimum character development without first understanding what comprises character. That would be tantamount to trying to build a better mousetrap without knowing what a mouse is. It would be nice if there were consensus on what is meant by the term character, but unfortunately, that is not the case. In common language, we use the term to mean either some measure of a person's goodness ("that really shows a lack of character on his part") or a person's eccentricity ("she is such a character!"). In both cases, the implication is that we are referring to some enduring characteristic of the person, although that is not always the case (his lack of character may be out of character for him).

The picture is even muddier when we examine how the term character is used technically. Some do not systematically distinguish between moral and nonmoral character, whereas others either restrict their definitions to the moral domain[1] or systematically separate moral from nonmoral aspects of character.[2] Even when these distinctions are

1. L. Kohlberg, *The Psychology of Moral Development, Essays on Moral Development, Vol.* 2 (New York: Harper and Row, 1984).

2. M. W. Berkowitz, "The Complete Moral Person: Anatomy and Formation" in J. M. DuBois, ed., *Moral Issues in Psychology: Personalist Contributions to Selected Problems* (Lanham, Md.: University Press of America, 1997): 11–42.

made, the criteria often differ; e.g., Nucci considers the moral domain to comprise universals,[3] whereas Lickona differentiates between universal and nonuniversal morality.[4] For some, character is pure personality, whereas for others it is mainly behavioral. Many omit cognitive functioning from their definitions of character. Some are comprehensive in their definitions, others not; some specific, others fairly global. I will not spend time here listing the differing definitions of character. I think you get the idea. Instead, I offer my own definition.

I define character as *an individual's set of psychological characteristics that affect that person's ability and inclination to function morally.* Simply put, character is comprised of those characteristics that lead a person to do the right thing or not to do the right thing. This serves as a global definition of character. Obviously, however, I still need to define what psychological characteristics affect moral functioning.

Elsewhere, I offer what I call the *Moral Anatomy.*[5] By this, I mean the psychological components that make up the complete moral person. There are seven parts to the moral anatomy: moral behavior, moral values, moral personality, moral emotion, moral reasoning, moral identity, and foundational characteristics. Whether one adopts this particular model of character or another (such as the tripartite model of cognition, affect, and behavior—head, heart, and hand—espoused by the Character Education Partnership and Lickona), the point to understand here is that character is a complex psychological concept.[6] It entails the capacity to think about right and wrong, experience moral emotions (guilt, empathy, compassion), engage in moral behaviors (sharing, donating to charity, telling the truth), believe in moral goods, demonstrate an enduring tendency to act with honesty, altruism, responsibility, and other characteristics that support moral functioning.

3. L. Nucci, *Education in the Moral Domain* (New York: Praeger, 2001).
4. T. Lickona, *Educating for Character* (New York: Bantam, 1991).
5. See M. W. Berkowitz, 1997.
6. See Lickona, 1991.

Just as Howard Gardner has redefined intelligence as a complex of psychological characteristics in his theory of multiple intelligences, I attempt to redefine character as a complex constellation of psychological dimensions of a person.

This perspective on character provides us with a road map through the following sections of this chapter. I am not wedded to this particular definition, but rather to defining character in a psychological, differentiated, and comprehensive manner. With this or another comprehensive, differentiated definition of character in hand, we can directly address how character develops and what can be done to foster or nurture its development.

Character Development

The recent epidemic of heinous acts of violence by children against children, such as the shooting of a young girl by a six-year-old boy in Flint, Michigan, has prompted many to raise the question of when character develops. This is a rather tricky question that I believe is fundamentally unanswerable. First, we have just established that character is a multifaceted phenomenon. Second, the components of character each have their own developmental trajectories. Third, each person develops at a different rate. Fourth, the developmental sequence and profile of the components of character differ in different individuals. Finally, the components of character tend to develop gradually, or in stages over a long period of time. Hence, we cannot state that the six-year-old boy in Flint did or did not have character. We cannot state either that six-year-olds in general do or do not have character. Rather, we can describe what aspects of character are typically developed (and to what degree) around six years of age. Then we can compare that child with what is typical, being careful to remember that children develop at different rates. For instance, if a six-year-old child showed no remorse over hurting another, did not realize that others may have perspectives different from his, or seemed not to care what others thought of him, we could then say that he seemed not to be developing some aspects of character that should be present at around his age.

Given this perspective, it is fair to claim that character begins developing at birth or even earlier. Because there is evidence of genetic influences on character, we can reasonably argue for prenatal character development. There is also evidence that parents begin to bond emotionally to a child even before birth, and we know that the bond between parent and infant is a critical factor in character development. It is well beyond the scope of this chapter to chronicle developments of all of the components of character development. Instead, I will illustrate its course by presenting developments of selected components in infancy, childhood, and adolescence (for a more detailed presentation, see Damon[7]).

Infant and Toddler Character Development

Some of the earliest, most significant hallmarks of the development of character are (1) the beginning of empathy, (2) the development of a concept of persons, and (3) the formation of the attachment bond. All of these begin during the first year of life.

Mature empathy entails self-awareness, self-other differentiation, perspective-taking, and the ability to draw inferences about the causes of another's distress. Martin Hoffman describes four stages of empathic development, the first of which covers most of the first year of life and the second of which begins at about nine or ten months of age. In the first stage the infant cries in response to another's crying, at first only very reflexively. (It is also around six months when the child develops a first sense of the other as separate from itself.) In the second stage, infants spend more time observing the other in distress and actively attempt to reduce their own resulting empathic distress (e.g., by thumb-sucking). This self-consoling behavior reveals the immaturity of empathy at this point; it is still focused on the self. Nevertheless, this is the

7. W. Damon, *The Moral Child* (New York: Free Press, 1988).

foundation of mature empathy, which is central to mature moral functioning or character.

The person concept refers to differentiation of self from other; that is, a recognition that you and I are separate entities with separate agency (independent capacities for causality) and separate existences. This begins to develop during the first two years of life. All character components (e.g., perspective-taking, moral reasoning, shame, cooperation) depend upon the development of self-other differentiation. It is impossible to be a moral agent without first recognizing that there are other human beings in the world.

The development of an attachment bond, the powerful emotional relationship that develops between an infant and his or her primary caretaker (typically mother), may be the single most important step in the development of character. The development begins roughly in the middle of the first year of life and evolves over the course of the life span. More important, however, it serves as a major influence on the nature of all future relationships. It has been linked to many other aspects of character such as peer cooperation, compliance with adults, and altruism. In fact, the absence of the motivation to have positive relationships with others (e.g., detachment, disinterest in social relationships) is a symptom of psychopathology, according to the American Psychiatric Association. The failure to form a secure attachment bond early in life may be the most significant cause of childhood antisocial behavior.

These diverse aspects of character (and others not described here) in the first two years of life are the foundation for later mature character and represent the first stages of character formation.

Childhood Character Development

So much of character develops during childhood that it is difficult to select a few examples for this discussion. Nevertheless, I will examine three: self-control, guilt, and perspective-taking.

Whereas self-control begins, in a sense, with the compliance of the toddler, the full capacity to regulate one's own impulses internally makes the greatest headway during the preschool years, especially between the ages of five and seven. Consequently, children are better able to delay gratification, control their impulses and aggressive urges, and direct their behavior. Roy Baumeister argues that self-control is a master virtue upon which other virtues depend.

Given the current interest in problems caused by children who seem not to have developed a conscience, the development of guilt feelings is of critical importance in understanding character development. Guilt is typically described as a self-critical emotional response to one's own transgressions. Thomas Lickona differentiates between constructive guilt (self-criticism leading to motivation for improvement) and destructive guilt (lowered self-esteem and self-denigration). For the development of character, we are clearly interested in the former. Grazyna Kochanska and her colleagues have found guilt feelings to increase significantly from two to three or four years after first emerging at about eighteen to twenty-four months.

Perspective-taking develops throughout the preschool and elementary school years, and its development continues throughout adolescence. There is some evidence that children as young as twenty-four to thirty months of age can do some rudimentary perspective-taking; however, the major advances in the capacity to understand others' points of view occur between three or four years and twelve years of age. Because moral functioning depends upon the ability to balance different people's interests, perspective-taking development is a critical foundational component of character. Clearly, key components of character become fully operative during the childhood years, making childhood a significant point for the transition to being a mature social and moral agent.

Adolescent Character Development

Most character development in adolescence is a continuation of what has already begun in infancy or childhood. I will examine the continued development of moral reasoning and the formation of a moral identity as two examples of adolescent character development.

Moral reasoning is the growth of the cognitive capacity to reason about matters of right and wrong, allowing for increasingly effective and mature moral decision-making and moral judgment. Moral reasoning is understood to develop in stages throughout the life span, beginning as young as three or four years of age. However, it is only at about eleven or twelve, as the child enters adolescence, that moral reasoning becomes predominantly prosocial, although the beginnings of such considerations are evident in the elementary school years. As children move through adolescence, their criteria for judging right and wrong shift from mostly self-oriented concerns with concrete consequences to themselves, to more socially oriented concerns with the impact of their behaviors on others, their relationships with others, and the social organizations of which they are members. The ability to figure out what is right and what is wrong is crucial as all people confront novel or ambiguous moral problems and true dilemmas. Furthermore, moral reasoning is related to a variety of moral and immoral behaviors such as altruism, cheating, delinquency, and risky behaviors (such as unsafe sexual practices and drug use).

Identity is the individual's self-constructed sense of self. Recent interest has turned to the concept of moral identity, the centrality of being good to one's self-concept, because of its appearance in studies of living and hypothetical moral exemplars. Adolescence is a critical time for the formation of a sense of self, an identity. Therefore, it is likely that the formation of a sense of oneself as a moral agent develops at the same time.

Sources of Character

If science can reveal what character is and how it develops, what can it tell us about how adults and society can actively promote the development of character in children? After all, it is up to adults and society to ensure that children have the opportunity to develop into competent moral adults, both for the sake of children and for the benefit of society. Family (especially parents) is typically considered the predominant influence on a child's character formation. Additionally, school, peers, community (including the media), religion, and biology are contributors.

It is clear that how parents raise a child is the predominant influence on the child's character formation. Some of the operative variables are parental affection, consistency of parenting, response to children's cues and signals, modeling, expression of values, respect for the child, and open discussion with the child. All aspects of children's character are impacted by these and other child-rearing factors.

School has an influence later than parenting because (1) parents are much more emotionally salient in the first years of life, and (2) many children do not experience full or even part-time schooling until they are three, four or five years of age, when, as we have just seen, many aspects of character are already developing. Schools can influence a child's self-concept (including self-esteem), social skills (especially peer social skills), values, moral reasoning maturity, prosocial inclinations and behavior, knowledge about morality, values, and so on.

The influence of peers begins in the preschool years, especially for children who attend preschools, but this influence clearly increases throughout childhood and peaks in adolescence. Peers have a strong effect on self-concept, social skills (e.g., conflict resolution, making and maintaining friendships), moral reasoning development, involvement in risky behaviors, and so on.

Community influences center around mass media exposure, neighborhood characteristics, and cultural values. Media clearly affect prejudice (racism, sexism, ageism), aggression, and sense of security. Religion has been related to lower risk behavior and greater mental health. The evidence about biology is much more controversial. Some argue for a strong genetic influence on aspects of character (altruism, risk-taking) and others suggest a much lesser role for genetics. Other biological factors have also been implicated, but only in extreme cases, such as in utero exposure to teratogens (such as opiates, alcohol) and serious disease factors.

Parenting and the Development of Character

Developmental psychology has much more to tell us about the effects of parenting on children's character development than other influences, including schooling. For that reason, John Grych and I examined the research literature for information about how parenting influences character development in children. What we discovered is that (1) much relevant research already exists, (2) a common core of parenting variables that promote character development can be identified from an empirical base, and (3) those parenting variables can also be applied to teacher behavior and character education.

We identified eight character variables extensively studied by developmental psychologists: social orientation (attachment), self-control, compliance, self-esteem, empathy, conscience, moral reasoning, and altruism. You will recognize some of these from the discussion above. We looked at what research has uncovered about the effect of parental behavior on the development of those eight character outcomes. We were able to identify five parenting behaviors that were significantly related to at least two of the eight character outcomes. *Responsivity/nurturance* was related to six of the eight outcomes (all but empathy and self-control). Parents who were responsive to children's signals and needs and had a warm, loving relationship with their children produced children of strong, multifaceted character. Families who used an open, democratic style of family discussion, decision-making, and problem-solving produced children who exhibited five characteristics (all but empathy, self-control, and social orientation). Parents who used *induction* (praising or disciplining with explanations that include a focus on the consequences of the child's behavior for other's feelings) produced children with relatively more mature empathy, conscience, altruism and moral reasoning. Parents who set high expectations (*demandingness*) that were attainable and supported, had children who were high in self-control, altruism, and self-esteem. Parents who *modeled* self-control and altruism had children high in self-control and altruism. Additional research will likely expand the list.

We can clearly mine the rich empirical literature in developmental psychology to better understand character development and what influences it. We know much about how parenting affects character and can easily apply this knowledge to schools, especially to teacher behavior.

What Works in Schools?

Few approaches to character education have been extensively researched. One of those, values clarification, has largely disappeared from the scene, in part due to generally ineffective scientific evidence. Extensive research on classroom dilemma discussion has demonstrated that it effectively promotes the development of moral reasoning capacities in students, and much is known about how it works. A detailed study of the Just Community Schools approach has demonstrated its effectiveness in promoting moral reasoning and stimulating the development of positive school culture and prosocial norms. The I-can-problem-solve approach to preventing impulsive and inhibited behaviors has been demonstrated repeatedly to be an effective means of reducing such behaviors in young school children.

The most extensive body of scientifically sound research about a comprehensive character education approach concerns the Child Development Project (a program of the Development Studies Center in Oakland, Calif., www.devstu.org). This elementary school reform program has been shown to promote prosocial behavior, reduce risky behaviors, stimulate academic motivation, create a positive school community, result in higher grades, and foster democratic values. Furthermore, it has identified the development of a caring school community as the critical mediating factor in the effectiveness of character education.

Numerous other character education initiatives and programs report single studies of effectiveness, but are not often reviewed and published. The best examples are the Responsive Classroom, Second Step, Positive Action, and the Resolving Conflict Creatively Program.

Solomon, Watson, and Battistich have compiled an extensive review of specific research studies about such programs and specific practices in implementing character education.[8] They conclude that four practices have strong empirical support for promoting character development: promoting student autonomy and influence; student participation, discussion, and collaboration; social skills training; and helping and social service behavior. An additional important mediating variable is moral atmosphere. The Child Development Project uses the term caring community and applies it both to the classroom and the entire school. The degree to which children perceive their schools as caring communities is directly related to the effectiveness of those schools in promoting student character development. Just Community Schools defines the variable somewhat differently, but reports that promotion of the development of moral atmosphere in the school is directly linked to the development of moral reasoning in students, and this finding has been internationally replicated. One solution to the lack of an empirical foundation on which to build a science of character education is to mine other fields for scientific evidence relevant to character education.

A fertile area to explore for relevant scientific research is risk-prevention. Alan Leschner, director of the National Institute on Drug Abuse, recently argued that prevention is generic and entails identifying those factors that protect against the risk factors that promote undesir-

8. D. Solomon, M. S. Watson and V. A. Battistich, "Teaching and Schooling Effects on Moral/Pro-Social Development" in V. Richardson, ed., *Handbook of Research on Teaching*, 4th ed. (Washington, D.C.: Association for Supervision and Curriculum Development, 2001).

able and dangerous behaviors. Other leaders in the field frequently echo this sentiment. Drug-use prevention researchers increasingly recognize that character-based interventions can effectively prevent substance use and abuse, just as character educators discover that their initiatives are preventive. Likewise, two of the most effective violence-prevention curricula, Second Step and Resolving Conflict Creatively, have been identified by the Character Education Partnership as character education initiatives. At the same time, the most effective character education program, the Child Development Project, is identified by the Department of Education as a model violence-prevention program and by the Center for Substance Abuse Prevention as a model prevention program. Others argue for the application of character education as a form of sex education. Furthermore, reviews of such tangentially related fields reveal striking parallels in what works.

Summary of What Works

Although much more research needs to be done to better understand what does and does not work, there is enough information available to reach some conclusions. The following represent seven rules of thumb for effective character education based on the research literature to date.

First, it is clear that the primary influence on a child's character development is *how people treat the child.* When schools focus on exhortations (PA announcements, posters, lecturers at special assemblies) or didactics (curriculum) as they are typically disposed to do, they miss the boat. To do effective character education, either in the home or the school, one has to focus on how people (especially those most significant to the child, but not only them) treat the child. What is the child's experience in spending a day in school? Is that child treated benevolently and with respect, or bullied or ignored? Does the child perceive school and classroom as nurturant, supportive places or as psychologically or physically toxic? Relationships are crucial to character development, so character education must focus on the quality of relationships in the school. This includes adult-to-child and child-to-child relationships. We can readily extrapolate from the parenting literature to adult and student relationships. Those relationships need to be benevolent (nurturant, supportive), authentic (honest, open), respectful (inclusive, valuing the student's voice), and consistent (predictable, stable). Most of the recent spate of school murders have implicated experiences of peer bullying as part of the cause of those horrors. Quality character education promotes prosocial relationships and caring school and classroom communities.

Second, we know that children learn, and their development is influenced by, what they observe, so the second principal factor in effective quality character education is *how significant others treat other people in the child's presence*, as Theodore and Nancy Sizer note in the title of their recent book *The Students Are Watching*. Parents are well aware that their children monitor and retain much of what they observe teachers and other adults in the school doing. Teachers are likewise well aware that students, even very young ones, report a wide variety of family behavior in the classroom. In both cases the observed and reported behaviors are often ones the adult models did not even realize were being registered or even observed, and in many cases they are behaviors they would rather were not observed at all and certainly not broadcast publicly. Students are indeed watching. What is worse is that they are also imitating. Elementary school teachers have taught me that if you want to know what kind of teacher you are, simply watch your students playing school. Modeling of positive behaviors such as altruism and empathy leads to such behavior in children. Modeling of undesirable behaviors such as violence and deceit similarly leads to the increase in those behaviors. It is pointless to expect children to be respectful and responsible if the adults in their lives do not act respectfully and responsibly. Many educators argue that they are not character educators and often that they do not want to be. If you work with or around children, *you cannot* not *be a character educator*. Abstaining is not an option. Your behavior will affect children's character development, for good or for ill. Cleaning up our acts and walking the talk is necessary for character education to be effective.

Third, schools need to *expect good character of all members*. In other words, character needs to be a clear priority and expectation—schools must demand good character. The expectations should be clear, they should be high but attainable, and there should be support structures to give students and other school members a reasonable chance of meeting those expectations. These expectations can come from a variety of sources, but ideally they come from the entire school community. All stakeholder groups should at least have some representation in the process of either generating or ratifying (if they come from another source) those expectations.

Previously, I stated that exhortations are not the primary means of affecting character development. There is nonetheless a place for *espousing positive character*. It serves two functions. First, it can reinforce what children learn and develop from watching and being treated positively by others. Secondly, it clarifies the often unclear messages of behavior. The powerful moral parenting behavior called induction works largely because it entails explanations of parent evaluative behavior (praising, chastising). So, as Thomas Lickona has taught us, we need not only to practice what we preach, but we also need to preach what we practice.

Children also need *opportunities to practice good character*. They need schools that promote student autonomy and influence. They need the opportunity to build skills such as perspective-taking, critical thinking, and conflict resolution, necessary for being a person of character. They also need opportunities to do good. Schools increasingly promote service activities of a variety of natures. Peer mediation, student self-governance, and charitable activities are examples of such opportunities.

To nurture the development of moral thinking capacities, students need *opportunities to reason about, debate, and reflect on moral issues*.

This includes opportunities to take others' perspectives, especially when those perspectives are different from one's own. This can be done within the curriculum, as in lessons and methods that promote student peer discussion of moral issues embedded in social studies and literature, or case studies in science or philosophy. It can also be done in stand-alone classes and programs that focus on issues of character and morality. The key is to create the kind of atmosphere in which students engage their peers to discuss such issues and in which they feel socially safe to do so honestly and forthrightly. Educators often need assistance in creating such an atmosphere, but that is essential for schools to effectively promote character development in students.

Finally, it is preferable if *parents are actively and positively involved in the school's character education efforts*. There is decidedly less scientific evidence to support this suggestion, but extrapolations from other areas of study clearly support the fact that parents will always be the primary influences on children's character development. Character education is most effective when schools and parents work in partnership.

Later Character Education

Thus far the analysis has been restricted to the typical years of elementary and secondary schooling, roughly ages six to eighteen, the kindergarten through high school years. Colleges and universities are also interested in contributing to the formation of character in the future citizens of our society. Having had the privilege of serving as the inaugural Ambassador Holland H. Coors Professor of Character Development at the United States Air Force Academy in 1999, I became very interested in what postsecondary education can offer to the character development of students. Lt. Colonel (Retired) Michael J. Fekula and I wrote an article detailing the principal components of postsecondary character education. They are:

- Teaching about character (morality, ethics)
- Displaying character (both by individuals and by the institution through its policies)
- Demanding character
- Practice in character (through apprenticeship, participation in school governance, community service, and experiential learning)
- Reflecting on character (verbally, in writing, and so on)

You will recognize many of these components from our prior discussion. However, what institutions like military academies and religiously affiliated colleges and universities (I spent twenty years teaching at Marquette University, a Jesuit institution in Milwaukee) bring to the table (at least potentially) is consistent, well-supported, and justified whole-institution commitment to character education. That is a remarkably valuable commodity in promoting character in schools and elsewhere.

Where Do We Go from Here?

Given the nascent state of the new "science of character education," many questions remain unanswered.

- What are the long-term effects of character education?
- Which components of comprehensive character education models impact which components of character?
- What are the most critical components of effective character education?
- How does effective character education vary from elementary to middle to high school?
- What is the overlap between effective character education and effective school-based prevention and service learning?

- How can we most effectively measure character?
- What is the "dose response" for effective character education; that is, how much is enough to make a difference?
- What existing forms of education impede the fostering of character?
- Must character education be schoolwide or can it be effectively implemented at the classroom level?

These are but a few important questions left for character scientists to answer. As more research is done, many more questions will surface. But if we work to develop a true science of character education, based on an empirical understanding of character development and those interventions that foster character development, then we will be well-armed to make a significant contribution, not only to our children, but to the world in which they and we live.

Moral Exemplarity

Lawrence J. Walker

THE FIELD OF moral psychology and moral education has stagnated seemingly, because of the conceptual skew and biases of dominant models. These models provide a threadbare conception of moral functioning and ineffectual means by which to foster children's moral development. I have two primary concerns. The first is that the field has been overly focused on moral rationality because of the influence of the formalist tradition in moral philosophy and the cognitive-developmental tradition in moral psychology with their aversion to personality factors, which they regard as corrupting influences on the purity of moral reason. The second concern is that the field has been preoccupied with the interpersonal aspects of morality that regulate our relationships with each other while ignoring the intrapsychic aspects that pertain more to our basic values, lifestyle, identity, and character. In this chapter I advocate a new direction for the field, stressing the development of moral personality, character, and virtue—a new direction that will be illustrated through the study of moral exemplarity.

Foundational to the present enterprise is some shared understanding of what is meant by "morality." Here I propose a working definition of morality and, in doing so, make explicit my own assumptions and understandings. I am quite aware of the recurrent controversies in moral philosophy regarding any such definition, and do not claim to have any resolution; I only intend to make clear my starting point. The definition is purposely broad, erring on the side of being overly inclusive rather than narrow. In my view, morality is a fundamental, pervasive aspect of human functioning, having both interpersonal and intrapersonal components. More specifically, it refers to voluntary actions that, at least potentially, have some social and interpersonal implications and that are governed by intrapsychic cognitive and emotive mechanisms.

There are a few things to note about this tentative definition. First, morality is clearly an interpersonal enterprise because it regulates people's interactions and adjudicates conflicts—it involves the impact of our behavior on others' rights and welfare. But morality is also an intrapersonal enterprise because it is integral to the how-shall-we-then-live existential question—it involves basic values, lifestyle, and identity. These intrapsychic aspects of moral functioning do have indirect implications for interpersonal interactions (as the above definition claims) because our values and moral character are played out in our relationships with others. The interpersonal aspects of moral functioning, with their focus on interpersonal rights and welfare, have been well represented in contemporary moral psychology and education but that has not been the case for the intrapsychic aspects. Dominant theories in moral psychology define the domain rather selectively and ignore issues of what has been pejoratively labeled private morality such as the development of the self and personal values.

The second thing about this definition of morality is that it claims that moral functioning is multifaceted, involving the dynamic interplay of thought, emotion, and behavior. Moral emotions such as guilt or empathy always occur with some accompanying cognitions, thoughts about one's personal values or one's interactions with others always entail some affect, and voluntary behaviors always have some basis in intentions that determine their moral quality. The interactive nature of moral functioning has been destructively minimized by the major theoretical traditions in the field, each of which has regarded different aspects of psychological functioning as representing the core of morality—the social-learning tradition has emphasized the acquisition of moral behaviors through principles of learning, the identification-internalization (psychoanalytic) tradition has emphasized the operation of moral emotions and defense mechanisms through the dynamics of identification with parents, and the cognitive-developmental tradition has emphasized the development of moral judgment through individuals' construction of meaning. This artificial trichotomy—represented by these major competing traditions in moral psychology—obfuscates the interdependent nature of thought, emotion, and behavior in moral functioning and trivializes our understanding by an exclusive focus on some particular component that has been hived off. A more comprehensive and holistic appreciation of how these different aspects relate to each other is a pressing goal for moral psychology.

These competing perspectives in moral psychology have not been meaningfully integrated and are somewhat out of balance. Taking poetic license, I contend that contemporary moral psychology has been afflicted by *rational planexia*—a condition of wandering astray, of being pulled out of proper [planetary] alignment by the "gravity" of moral rationality. Moral psychology, like so many other disciplines within the social sciences and beyond, has been inordinately influenced by the legacy of the Enlightenment which, among other things, was concerned with establishing a rational basis for moral understandings and convictions to overcome the perils of ethical relativism. Note that this preoccupation with the rational foundations for morality supplanted the centuries-old ethical concern with moral virtues and character (the Aristotelian tradition), the concern that perhaps better accords with commonsense notions of moral life.

The dominant philosophical perspective girdling the field has been the formalist tradition, best exemplified by Immanuel Kant, with its assumptions emphasizing individualism, justice, rights, and duties. Kant holds a dualistic view of human nature—reason versus passion—with rationality forming the core of moral functioning and personological factors (emotions, desires, personal projects, and so on) regarded with much suspicion, as corrupting biases to overcome if people are to attain to the standard of autonomous moral rationality.

Similarly, the prevailing psychological framework in moral psychology has been the structuralist cognitive-developmental tradition, exemplified by Lawrence Kohlberg, with its assumptions emphasizing the stage-like development of moral reasoning abilities. The structuralist tradition has not been alone in this cognitive emphasis. Psychology, in general, has been subjected to a veritable cognitive revolution as psychoanalytic and behavioral theories have been eclipsed by cognitive and information-processing approaches, reflecting the liberal optimism that arose in the period following the Second World War. Kohlberg can be credited with overcoming much of the philosophical naïveté of early research on morality and with establishing moral development as a legitimate field of psychological inquiry.[1] His model has dominated moral psychology for almost three decades, and perhaps rightly so, for his conceptual, empirical, and applied contributions have been monumental. Few would quibble with that claim, and even people who disagree with Kohlberg frequently rely on his theory as a foil. Their responses are often framed by the fundamental assumptions undergirding his model, illustrating its profound influence. Kohlberg's formalist and structuralist heritage led him to focus on moral reasoning development, assessed through individuals' cerebrated resolution of moral quandaries. He seeks to establish an account of moral development defined by reason and revealed through the developmental process. He argues that moral conflicts are best resolved through principles of justice

1. See L. Kohlberg, *Essays on Moral Development, Vol. 1, The Philosophy of Moral Development* (San Francisco: Harper & Row, 1981) and *Vol. 2, The Psychology of Moral Development* (San Francisco: Harper & Row, 1984).

and that such reasoning is auto-motivating, sufficient to compel moral action (here Kohlberg adopts Plato's two maxims, "virtue is one and its name is justice" and "to know the good is to do the good").

But these assumptions have hardly gone unchallenged: other competing conceptions of the good besides justice, such as care and community, have been advocated and the predictability of action on the basis of moral judgment is rather tenuous, pointing to the "gappiness" of moral life. Furthermore, Kohlberg's vision of moral maturity centers on principled moral judgment, an ideal ethical standpoint requiring abstract impartiality as we separate ourselves from our own personalities and interests to follow the dictates of universalizable moral principles—a vision of moral maturity that is rather psychologically barren and suspect. The philosophical constraints and psychological emphases inherent in Kohlberg's model have the inevitable consequence of restriction of perspective, a conceptual skew that results in a narrow view of moral functioning. Kohlberg was not entirely blind to the constraints placed on his model by the emphasis on moral rationality and justice, and he attempted to flesh out his theory in several ways, at least as much as his theoretical allegiances would allow; but the model could only be tweaked so far and its core emphasis on cognition and justice remained.

Other influential theorists in moral psychology[2] have also implicitly assumed the objectives of modernity and so can be similarly tarred and feathered for their emphasis on moral rationality and minimal attention

2. N. Eisenberg, "Prosocial Development: A Multifaceted Model," in W. M. Kurtines and J. L. Gewirtz, eds., *Moral Development: An Introduction* (Boston: Allyn & Bacon, 1995); C. Gilligan, *In a Different Voice: Psychological Theory and Women's Development* (Cambridge, Mass.: Harvard University Press, 1982); J. R. Rest, D. Narvaez, M. J. Bebeau, and S. J. Thoma, *Postconventional Moral Thinking: A Neo-Kohlbergian Approach* (Mahwah, N.J.: Erlbaum, 1999); R. A. Shweder, M. Mahapatra, and J. G. Miller, "Culture and Moral Development, " in J. Kagan and S. Lamb, eds., *The Emergence of Morality in Young Children* (Chicago: University of Chicago Press, 1987): 1–83; E. Turiel, *The Development of Social Knowledge: Morality and Convention* (Cambridge, England: Cambridge University Press, 1983).

to moral personality, character, and intuition.[3] The alignment of the moral psychology field in general has been skewed by this pervasive emphasis on moral rationality in its application to interpersonal functioning.

This prevailing emphasis on moral rationality has eclipsed attention to other aspects of moral functioning and has belied the complexity of the moral life. The danger of this overemphasis on moral rationality is that it separates people from their own personalities and risks destroying their motivation to be moral—a situation that has been labeled moral schizophrenia.[4] A slightly different way to articulate this concern is to note moral psychology's preoccupation with the interpersonal aspects of moral functioning (justice, rights, welfare, care) and its relative neglect of the intrapsychic aspects that involve the characteristics of the good person and the good life (basic values, identity, integrity). Flanagan similarly critiques the marginalization of moral character in philosophy and argues convincingly for a more realistic conception of moral functioning and moral ideals—one that is psychologically possible for "creatures like us." Flanagan does not regard current ethical frameworks as very useful for informing moral action because they presuppose psychological functioning that is impossible for ordinary people ever to attain.

> Any moral theory must acknowledge that . . . the projects and commitments of particular persons give each life whatever meaning it has; and that all persons, even very impartial ones, are partial to their own projects. It follows that no ethical conception . . . can reasonably

3. R. L. Campbell and J. C. Christopher, "Moral Development Theory: A Critique of Its Kantian Presuppositions," *Developmental Review* 16 (1996): 1–47; J. Haidt, "The Emotional Dog and Its Rational Tail: A Social Intuitionist Approach to Moral Judgment," *Psychological Review* (in press); D. K. Lapsley, *Moral Psychology* (Boulder, Colo.: Westview Press, 1996) and "An Outline of a Social-Cognitive Theory of Moral Character," *Journal of Research in Education* 8 (1998): 25–32.

4. M. Stocker, "The Schizophrenia of Modern Ethical Theories," *Journal of Philosophy* 73 (1976): 453–66.

> demand a form of impersonality, abstraction, or impartiality which ignores the constraints laid down by universal psychological features.[5]

Thus, we hear increasingly frequent appeals to enrich the psychological study of moral development by integrating cognition with personality and character, thereby providing more holistic understandings of moral functioning and effective means to foster moral development. It is important to note that these criticisms of the rationalistic bias of contemporary moral psychology do not negate the essential role that moral reasoning plays; rather these concerns argue for a more full-bodied and balanced account of moral functioning that meaningfully includes moral personality and character.

New Directions for Moral Psychology: Personality and Character

The new direction that seems to be evolving in the psychology of moral development is the study of moral personality and character, an approach that has the potential to include both the inter- and intrapersonal aspects of moral functioning as well as encompass the cognitive, affective, and behavioral components. Similarly, recognition is beginning among moral philosophers of the need to constrain ethical theories by an empirically informed account of how people ordinarily understand morality, as well as by the psychological processes involved in moral functioning.[6]

What I advocate, and pursue in my own empirical work, is a two-pronged approach to developing such an integrated account of moral functioning: One approach examines people's conceptions of moral

5. O. Flanagan, *Varieties of Moral Personality: Ethics and Psychological Realism* (Cambridge, Mass.: Harvard University Press, 1991): 100–101.

6. See especially M. L. Johnson, "How Moral Psychology Changes Moral Theory," in L. May, M. Friedman, and A. Clark, eds., *Minds and Morals: Essays on Cognitive Science and Ethics* (Cambridge, Mass.: MIT Press, 1996): 45–68.

functioning and moral excellence, notions that are embedded in everyday language and common understandings, the other the psychological functioning of moral exemplars, people who have been identified as leading lives of moral virtue, integrity, and commitment. These different empirical strategies should be mutually informative, providing convergent evidence regarding aspects of moral functioning that are operative in everyday life and should be incorporated into our theories of moral development and approaches to moral education and socialization.

Conceptions of Moral Excellence

Part of the impetus for examining people's conceptions of moral excellence is to address the skew that dominant models of moral psychology have introduced through various biases and prior assumptions. Philosophical perspectives have the inherent potential to limit and need to be checked against the empirical evidence yielded by ordinary understanding and intuition. At this juncture, moral psychology and education need to be more closely aligned with how people experience morality day by day than by the tight constraints of philosophical conceptualizations. My hunch is that a broad survey of conceptions of moral functioning may reveal some important notions that have been sidelined in contemporary moral psychology because of the encumbrance of philosophical and methodological blinders.

This new direction in moral psychological research is illustrated through the findings of a recent project in which I examined people's conceptions of moral excellence.[7] Although most theories of moral development accord minimal attention to definitions of moral exemplarity, Kohlberg did articulate an explicit vision of moral maturity—the attainment of dilemma-busting principles of justice—but as argued before, this view is an impoverished and psychologically barren one

7. L. J. Walker and R. C. Pitts, "Naturalistic Conceptions of Moral Maturity," *Developmental Psychology* 34 (1998): 403–19.

because of its focus on moral rationality. Regardless, there is scant empirical evidence for the elusive Stage 6 (universal ethical principles). We need a more compelling and full-bodied conception of moral excellence. My research on conceptions of moral excellence entailed a sequence of three studies (using free-listing, prototypicality-rating, and similarity-sorting procedures) and was intended to provide a handle on people's implicit notions and typologies of morality. Analyses identified two dimensions underlying people's understanding of moral maturity: a self–other dimension and an external–internal dimension. The self–other dimension incorporates some of the dynamics of the notions of dominance and nurturance (or agency and communion) as fundamental in the understanding of interpersonal behavior, and illustrates the tension between notions of personal agency and communion in moral functioning. The external–internal dimension reflects the tension between external moral standards and a personal conscience. This implies that moral maturity requires both sensitivity to shared moral norms and development of autonomous moral values and standards.

Analyses also identified clusters of attributes (or themes) in people's understanding of moral maturity. The principled–idealistic cluster reflects the importance of a range of strongly held values and principles and the maintenance of high standards and ideals—an acute and evident sense of morality. The fair cluster entails the notions of justice, principle, and rationality that reflect Kohlberg's conception of moral excellence, so naturalistic conceptions do include that component of morality. The dependable–loyal and caring–trustworthy clusters resonate with themes of interpersonal sensitivity and warmth. Thus, other-oriented compassion and care that entail helpful and considerate action, as well as the nurturing of relationships through faithfulness and reliability, are significant in notions of moral functioning. The confident cluster references the qualities of agency that are important in the pursuit of moral goals. The strong commitment to moral values and standards (principled–idealistic cluster) joined with a strong sense of self and agency (confident cluster) may contribute to the integrity that is viewed as essential to moral maturity (has integrity cluster)—that the moral person is committed to action based on these principles, values, and ideals, and has the personal fortitude to do so.

Among the moral virtues emphasized here were notions of honesty, truthfulness, and trustworthiness, as well as those of care, compassion, thoughtfulness, and considerateness. Other salient traits revolve around virtues of dependability, loyalty, and conscientiousness. These aspects of moral character are foundational for interpersonal relationships and social functioning, but have received scant attention in moral psychology or have been relegated to an immature good-boy-girl mentality. Finally, the notion of integrity is at the core of the depiction of moral excellence. Integrity represents the connection between thought and action, but both the rationalistic and behavioral models of moral functioning have been unable to escape their own parameters and, thus, the notion of integrity has fallen into the void when instead it should be basic both to our understanding of moral psychology and attempts to nurture its development.

This notion of integrity and the development of a moral self is, however, receiving increasing attention in moral psychology and moral philosophy.[8] Blasi advocates the notion of a moral self that reflects how people conceptualize the moral domain and the extent to which morality is salient and significant in their self-concept and identity. Research with moral exemplars points to the exceptional merger of self and morality in their lives, with little distinction between personal and

8. A. Blasi, "Moral Understanding and the Moral Personality: The Process of Moral Integration," in W. M. Kurtines and J. L. Gewirtz, eds., *Moral Development: An Introduction* (Boston: Allyn & Bacon, 1995): 229–53; G. G. Noam and T. E. Wren, eds., *The Moral Self* (Cambridge, Mass.: MIT Press, 1993); V. A. Punzo, "After Kohlberg: Virtue Ethics and the Recovery of the Moral Self," *Philosophical Psychology* 9 (1996): 7–23; L. J. Walker and K. H. Hennig, "Moral Development in the Broader Context of Personality," in S. Hala, ed., *The Development of Social Cognition* (East Sussex, England: Psychology Press, 1997): 297–327.

moral goals,[9] and with self-attributions that predominantly include moral personality traits and goals.[10] Also in Blasi's model are the notions of personal responsibility for moral action and of self-consistency or integrity. Obviously, moral psychology requires a systematic empirical examination of the role of the self in moral functioning, as it has the potential to link the cognitive and emotive aspects of moral functioning to behavior. An example of such work is Bandura's research on the self-regulating affective processes that are sometimes deactivated in the context of one's own questionable conduct.[11] Given people's strong need to regard themselves as moral, Bandura notes the corrupting power of rationalizations in laundering evaluations of behavior to preserve this sense of the moral self (through reconstruals, euphemistic labeling, advantageous comparisons, displacement of responsibility). The greater self-awareness and self-consistency of moral maturity should help to inhibit such moral disengagement.

There are some difficulties with virtue ethics, in general, that need to be kept front and center as the field moves in this new direction. For example, a listing of moral virtues, such as was done in this study, represents an amalgamation of traits that would be impossible, indeed incoherent, for any one person to embody. At present, we little understand how these aspects of moral character interact in psychological functioning. Lapsley has noted that not all virtues are necessarily compatible: "Certain characterological blindspots might be the price one pays for cultivating excellences in other domains of one's life."[12] An

9. A. Colby and W. Damon, *Some Do Care: Contemporary Lives of Moral Commitment* (New York: Free Press, 1992).

10. D. Hart and S. Fegley, "Prosocial Behavior and Caring in Adolescence: Relations to Self-Understanding and Social Judgment," *Child Development* 66 (1995): 1346–59.

11. A. Bandura, "Social Cognitive Theory of Moral Thought and Action," in W. M. Kurtines and J. L. Gewirtz, eds., *Handbook of Moral Behavior and Development, Vol. 1* (Hillsdale, N.J.: Erlbaum, 1991): 45–103.

12. See Lapsley, 1998: 32.

illustration in this regard comes from Colby and Damon's study of moral exemplars who were identified largely on the basis of their commitment to moral causes (in other words, most were social activists).[13] Many exemplars expressed regrets regarding relationships with their children who sometimes seemed to lose out in competition with their parents' pursuit of social causes.

On a related theme, it also needs to be recognized that virtues sometimes have maladaptive, or at least morally questionable, aspects to their expression. Hennig and Walker used techniques of personality assessment to map the ethic-of-care domain.[14] We focused on aspects of the virtue of care where it has in some sense gone awry, being dysfunctional for either the carer or the one cared for. Self-sacrificial care can justify self-neglect and overinvolvement in others' lives, and thus compromise the quality of care undertaken. Another maladaptive pattern identified was submissive care, where care for the other is anxiously motivated by fear of negative evaluation and where one's self-expression is inhibited in deference to others' opinions. In other words, the virtue of caring can take on less than authentic manifestations. This is presumably true for most virtues, and moral psychology would be served well by a careful conceptual and empirical analysis along these lines of other moral traits.

It should be obvious that there may be no single viable prototype for moral maturity or ideal of moral character; indeed, there may be many different types of moral excellence and moral exemplars. My current research explores conceptions of different types of moral excellence that may reveal the clusters of virtues associated with different types as well as reveal the virtues that are seen as foundational to all manifestations of moral maturity. That there are many different types

13. See Colby and Damon, 1992.

14. K. H. Hennig and L. J. Walker, *Mapping the Care Domain: A Structural and Substantive Analysis.* Manuscript submitted for publication, University of British Columbia, 2001.

of moral exemplars is illustrated by the findings of a study where participants were asked to identify moral exemplars and to justify their choices.[15] A wide range of moral exemplars was identified, including humanitarians, revolutionaries, social activists, religious leaders, politicians, and so on. However, the most frequent categories were family members and friends. Many participants expressed an explicit distrust of the public persona of historical figures, preferring to nominate individuals they knew intimately and were better able to evaluate. There are a couple of notable things here: First, that a great diversity of moral exemplars was identified; and second, that many moral exemplars would not be considered well-known. Analysis of the justifications for these nominations revealed that actual moral exemplars are not typically described as having a full complement of moral virtues but rather are seen as embodying a smaller subset (think of Oskar Schindler vs. Martin Luther King vs. Mother Teresa), suggesting the need for us to understand better the complex interrelationships among these aspects of moral character and how they are manifested. Of course, these naturalistic conceptions of moral maturity need to be checked against analyses of the psychological functioning of actual moral exemplars. Do real moral paragons actually evidence the range of attributes derived from natural language concepts? It is to this complementary avenue of research that we now turn.

Psychological Functioning of Moral Exemplars

Another way to examine the development of moral character and personality is through comprehensive analyses of the psychological functioning of people who have been identified as leading morally exemplary lives. In a landmark study that frames our own research in some

15. L. J. Walker, R. C. Pitts, K. H. Hennig, and M. K. Matsuba, "Reasoning about Morality and Real-Life Moral Problems," in M. Killen and D. Hart, eds., *Morality in Everyday Life: Developmental Perspectives* (Cambridge: Cambridge University Press, 1995): 371–407.

respects, Colby and Damon studied a sample of people who evidenced extraordinary commitment to moral ideals and causes over an extended period of time.[16] Their case-study analysis revealed that these exemplars were not particularly distinguished in terms of principled moral reasoning, again challenging the dominant prototype for moral maturity, but they were characterized by other processes suggestive of various aspects of the moral personality, including: (a) active receptivity to progressive social influence and a continuing capacity to change, (b) considerable certainty about moral principles and values which was balanced by relentless truth-seeking and openmindedness (precluding dogmatism), (c) positivity and optimism, humility (with a disavowal of moral courage), love for all people, a capacity to forgive, and an underlying faith or spirituality, and (d) an exceptional uniting of self and morality, reflecting an identity that fused the personal and moral aspects of their lives (as noted earlier in the discussion of the moral self). They saw moral problems in everyday events and saw themselves as implicated in these problems and responsible to act. Despite these valuable insights, it should be noted that this was a small, select sample with no comparison group, the method was assisted autobiographical interview with no standard measures of psychological functioning, and the analyses were solely qualitative.

The value of analyses of the psychological functioning of moral exemplars in suggesting processes underlying the development of moral personality and character can be further demonstrated through the findings of another recent project, a study that we believe provides one of the more comprehensive assessments of moral exemplarity.[17] An exemplar group of forty young adults was nominated by social service

16. See Colby and Damon, 1992.

17. M. K. Matsuba and L. J. Walker, *Caring for Their Community: Study of Moral Exemplars in Transition to Adulthood.* Manuscript in preparation, University of British Columbia, 2001.

agencies because of their extraordinary moral commitment as volunteers, and a matched comparison group was also recruited. Participants completed several questionnaires and responded to a lengthy life-narrative interview. In an attempt to provide a comprehensive assessment of individuals' psychological functioning, the choice of measures here reflected McAdams' typology of three broad levels of personality assessment: (a) dispositional traits, (b) contextualized concerns such as developmental tasks and personal strivings, and (c) integrative narratives of the self.[18] In terms of dispositional traits, participants completed a questionnaire assessing traits reflecting the five fundamental factors underlying personality. Of the five factors, agreeableness and conscientiousness are considered the classic dimensions of character and thus most relevant here. Not surprisingly, the exemplar group was found to be higher on agreeableness than the comparison group, confirming that personality dispositions are implicated in moral action.

To assess the midlevel of contextualized concerns in understanding personality functioning, we included various measures of developmental tasks and personal strivings. It was found that, in contrast to the comparison group, the exemplar group was more mature in their identity, reflecting a stronger commitment to values and greater stability; they evidenced more mature faith development, reflecting the process by which they make meaning in life; and they used more advanced moral reasoning, confirming its critical role in moral functioning.

At the third level of personality assessment we examined themes in individuals' life narratives. Our expectation was that exemplars' life narratives would by characterized by more themes of agency and communion than would be evident for the comparison individuals. Our hunch was partly supported in that more agentic themes were found in exemplars' life stories. This finding resonates with the results of our

18. D. P. McAdams, "What Do We Know When We Know a Person?" *Journal of Personality* 63 (1995): 365–96.

previous study that identified personal agency as a salient dimension underlying understandings of moral excellence.[19]

In summarizing our research on moral exemplars, we found that variables indicative of all three levels of personality assessment distinguished exemplars from comparison individuals (despite matching on demographic variables). Yet, we need to keep in mind that moral maturity can be exemplified in different ways, and it is important for our understanding of moral functioning to determine what is distinctive about different types of moral exemplars as well as the common core. We currently have research underway along these lines. Once the field shows some sense of the psychological functioning of moral exemplars, the research agenda may then focus on the formative factors in the development of such moral character.

Applications and Conclusions

My premise in this chapter is that progress in moral psychology and moral education has stalled because of the conceptual skew of the models of moral development that dominate the field with their focus on moral rationality and aversion to personological factors, and the resultant psychologically barren conception of moral functioning. Furthermore, their emphasis has been on the interpersonal aspects of morality, while ignoring the intrapsychic aspects that pertain more to our basic values, lifestyle, identity, and character.

The new direction advocated here is intended as a corrective to this misalignment and stresses the development of moral personality, character, and virtue, a new direction that can perhaps best be instanced through the study of moral exemplarity. This approach has the potential to include both the inter- and intrapersonal aspects of morality because moral character and virtues are reflected in our relationships. It also has the potential to integrate the cognitive, affective, and behavioral com-

19. See Walker and Pitts, 1998.

ponents of moral functioning, because the notion of moral character is not so amenable to this psychological trichotomy and implicates all in its manifestations. This new direction resonates with recent appeals for the study of positive human characteristics and the experiences that foster such behaviors—what is known as the positive psychology movement.[20]

An initial two-pronged empirical approach to the study of moral exemplarity is described and illustrated. One approach is to examine conceptions of moral excellence, rooted in everyday language and common understandings, as an avenue to a broad understanding of moral virtues and ideals. The other approach is to examine the actual psychological functioning of individuals identified as moral exemplars, using the template of the most valid models and measures of human development. It is anticipated that these two approaches will yield convergent evidence regarding moral functioning and ideals; their points of divergence will require some rethinking of our notions. The beginning research along these lines has implications for our engagement in moral education with our children and youth. Perhaps pivotal is the need to sensitize children to the breadth of the moral domain and the moral implications of their values, choices, and actions. Morality should be considered a pervasive part of everyday life and should be front-and-center in our thinking. Making children more aware of the moral domain will facilitate the development of a moral identity where moral concerns become relevant to most things undertaken in life.

Moral education should also entail a critical discussion of moral virtues. Simply plastering the classroom walls with virtue labels will do little, if anything, to engender good moral character; rather, children need to appreciate the complexities and perhaps even the maladaptive aspects of many virtues such as honesty and care, and to struggle daily with how to exemplify these virtues. Some illustrations may help to

20. M. E. P. Seligman and M. Csikszentmihalyi, "Positive Psychology: An Introduction," *American Psychologist* 55(2000): 5–14.

demonstrate my point here regarding the complexity and shadowy side of many virtues. The virtue of honesty needs to be tempered by considerations of avoiding hurt to others, as when responding to grandma's query about whether you liked the sweater she knit for you (when the sweater is hopelessly out of style). Likewise, the virtue of care can be maladaptive when excessive caring for others is based on self-denigration and -denial and simply results in a resentful sense of obligation in others. Children need to appreciate that appropriate care depends on maintaining an authentic sense of self. Other virtues often also come into conflict, and those situations need to be carefully considered; for example, when loyalty to a friend is challenged by a teacher's interrogation about cheating in the classroom. The notion of moral exemplarity means that such moral examples are worthy of some emulation. Children need to explore the lives of a range of moral exemplars. Certainly, some well-known historical and publicly visible exemplars need to be examined; but also, the lives of local and personal heroes should be included. Here it is important that lives in all their fullness are examined, not just heroes' statements or actions, but rather the complexity of their personalities, the formative aspects of their experiences, and their weaknesses and struggles. It is important for children to recognize the diversity in moral exemplarity and to identify with a personal hero. Children should not simply cognitively study moral exemplars, but their involvement in moral action should be facilitated. The recent emphasis on meaningful community service involvement reflects this idea.

Finally, children need to struggle with underlying tensions in moral functioning, as were described earlier in our research. For example, one dimension underlying notions of morality is the self–other dimension that involves the notions of agency and communion. Here there is a need to balance the development of competency with interpersonal sensitivity, sometimes a difficult equilibrium to maintain in many moral situations. The development of children's commitment to moral values and their willingness to act on them needs to be balanced by openness to new ideas and sensitivity to the perspectives and circumstances of others. The danger is that we can instill such a sense of personal agency and moral certainty in children that they run roughshod over others in their pursuit of their own moral goals. Another dimension underlying notions of morality is the external–internal dimension that reflects the frequent tension between shared moral norms and autonomous moral principles. Here again, children need to appreciate the occasional tension between respect for the moral values of one's community and the need to follow carefully considered individual moral ideals and principles. Certainly, there are many possibilities to consider and evaluate as we chart new directions in moral psychology and moral education.

Educating the Stoic Warrior

Nancy Sherman

IN A REMARKABLY prescient moment, James B. Stockdale, then a senior Navy pilot shot down over Vietnam, muttered to himself as he parachuted into enemy hands, “Five years down there, at least. I’m leaving behind the world of technology and entering the world of Epictetus.”[1] Epictetus’s famous handbook, the *Enchiridion*, was Stockdale’s bedtime reading in the many carrier wardrooms he occupied as he cruised in the waters off Vietnam in the mid-sixties. Stoic philosophy resonated with Stockdale’s temperament and profession, and he committed many of Epictetus’s pithy remarks to memory. Little did he know on that shoot-down day of Septemer 9, 1965, that Stoic tonics would hold the key to his survival for six years of POW life. They would also form the

1. From James B. Stockdale, *Courage Under Fire: Testing Epictetus’s Doctrines in a Lab of Human Behavior* (Stanford: Hoover Institution Press, 1994).

backbone of his leadership style as the senior officer in the POW chain of command.

It doesn't take too great a stretch of the imagination to think of a POW survivor as a kind of Stoic sage, for the challenge the POW lives with is the Stoic's challenge: to find dignity when stripped of nearly all nourishment of the body and soul. Stoicism is a philosophy of defense, a philosophy of "sucking it up." On a strict reading, it minimizes vulnerability by denying the intrinsic goodness of things that lie outside one's control. In many ways, boot camp is a green soldier's early lesson in Stoicism. In general, it is easy to think of military men and women as Stoics. The very term has come to mean, in our vernacular, controlled, disciplined, not easily agitated or disturbed. Military officers tend to cultivate these character traits. In a vivid way, they live out the consolations of Stoic practical philosophy. In this paper I explore certain aspects of military moral education by returning to ancient Stoic teachings.

My own tour of duty with the military began on a drizzly February day in 1994. A Navy chaplain had invited me to brainstorm with the top brass about moral remediation for some 133 midshipmen implicated in an "EE" or "double E" (electrical engineering) cheating scandal. The chaplain knew I was no Navy insider, but he wanted my input as an academic ethicist. That February meeting in 1994 led initially to a consultancy and visiting ethics lectureship whose audience was the implicated EE students. Then, in 1997, I was appointed the inaugural Distinguished Chair in Ethics at the Naval Academy. I was brought aboard, in naval lingo, to teach what American and European universities had been teaching for the better part of this century—essentially, Ethics 101. But at an engineering school like the Naval Academy, introductory ethics had passed them by. Leadership courses were a standard mix of management and motivational psychology. Yet the far more ancient subject of ethics was somehow viewed as a newfangled, possibly heretical course that would dare to teach what ought to be bred in the bones. I was to teach ethics, ethics for the military. That was contractual. What wasn't prearranged was what the military would teach me. They would allow me entrance into a world that for many of my generation had been cut off by Vietnam and had remained largely impregnable ever since. And they would offer something of a living example of the doctrines of Stoicism I had studied before only as texts.

The allure of Stoicism became explicit each term at a certain point in the semester. The course I taught covered topical themes of honesty, liberty, virtue, and just war interwoven with the writings of historical figures such as Aristotle and Aquinas, John Stuart Mill and Immanuel Kant, and Epictetus as a representative Stoic. It was when we arrived at Epictetus that many felt they had come home. What resonated with them was what resonated with Jim Stockdale as he read Epictetus each night.

> There are things which are within our power, and there are things which are beyond our power. Within our power are opinion, aim, desire, aversion, and in one word, whatever affairs are our own. Beyond our power are body, property, reputation, office, and in one word, whatever are not properly our own affairs.
>
> . . . Remember, then, that if you attribute freedom to things by nature dependent and take what belongs to others for your own, you will be hindered, you will lament, you will be disturbed, you will find fault both with gods and men . . . If it concerns anything beyond our power, be prepared to say that it is nothing to you.[2]

Epictetus rightly thinks that our opinions, desires, and emotions are in our power, not in the radical sense that we can produce them, instantly, at will, but in the sense that we can do things, indirectly, to shape them. He is right to think, with the Stoics in general, that our opinions about self and others influence our desires and emotions. In contrast to these things over which we have some control, we have far less control over other sorts of goods. A marine may be killed in friendly fire that he had no way of avoiding, a sailor may be deserving of deco-

2. *Enchiridion*, Hackett, trans. (Indianapolis: N. White, 1983): 11.

ration and promotion, though overlooked because of gender prejudice that she alone can't change, stocks may take a nosedive however prudent one's investments. A Stoic, like Epictetus, reminds us of the line that divides what is and what is not within our control and that we will be miserable if our happiness itself depends too heavily upon things over which we have little dominion. The Stoic recommendation is not complacency or a retreat to a narrow circle of safety. We are to continue to meet challenges and take risks, to stretch the limits of our mastery. We are to continue to strive with our best efforts to achieve our ends, but we must learn greater strength in the face of what we simply cannot change.

A Brave New Stoicism

Who are the Stoics from whom the military take implicit guidance? Epictetus has been mentioned, but we need to put his writings in historical context. Roughly speaking, the ancient Stoics span the period from 300 B.C. to A.D. 200. They are part of the broad Hellenistic movement of philosophy that follows upon Aristotle and includes, in addition to Stoicism, ancient Skepticism and Epicureanism. The early Greek Stoics, known as the old Stoa (taking their name from the *stoa* or painted colonnade near the central piazza of Athens where disciples paced back and forth) were interested in systematic philosophical thought that joined ethics with studies in physics and logic. The works of the founders of the school—Zeno, Cleanthes, and Chrysippus—survive only in fragments, quoted by later writers. Indeed, much of what we know about Stoicism comes through Roman redactors such as Cicero, Seneca, Epictetus, and Marcus Aurelius. These Roman redactors, some writing in Greek—Epictetus and Marcus Aurelius—others writing in Latin—Seneca and Cicero—viewed themselves as public philosophers at the center of public life.

Cicero (106–43 B.C.), well-known Roman political orator, consul, and ally to Pompey, turned to specifically philosophical writing at the end of his political career after Caesar's assassination (which Cicero viewed as a tyrannicide) and while in hiding from his own future assassins, Antony and the other triumvirs. Though himself not a Stoic (rather he identified as a member of the New Academy or school of Skepticism), he wrote extensively on Stoic views and his work, especially *On Ends* and *On Duties*, remained highly influential throughout the Renaissance and Enlightenment as statements of Stoic positions. Seneca, writing in the mid-first century A.D., was the tutor and political adviser of the young emperor, Nero. He wrote voluminously on, among other things, the passions and how anger, hatred, and envy, if not understood and properly reined in, can ruin a ruler and bring down a commonwealth, as well as about attachment and fortune, and how we can learn to become less vulnerable to their vicissitudes. Epictetus, a Greek slave-turned-philosopher who also wrote in the time of Nero's reign, greatly influenced Marcus Aurelius. Epictetus's aphoristic writings, summarized in a popular handbook, teach about the power of our minds and imagination to find a measure of mastery and fulfillment even in enslavement.

Marcus Aurelius, a Roman emperor and warrior, wrote his famous *Meditations* in A.D. 172 in the fleeting moments of quiet he was able to snatch during German campaigns. In contrast to Seneca's writings, which are often addressed to others, Marcus's meditations are exhortations to himself, about his status as a citizen of the world and the community of humanity and god linked through reason and law with nature. He warns how one can be lured away from reason by the attractions of place or wealth or pleasurable indulgence, and how a zeal for glory can pervert happiness. A repeated theme is that we live in a Heraclitean world of flux. To find happiness, we cannot hold on too tightly to what is transient and beyond our control.

The Stoics teach self-sufficiency and the importance of detaching from dependence on worldly goods that make us vulnerable. In a similar fashion, they advocate detachment from sticky emotions that mark our investment in things beyond our control. In a manner of speaking, the soldier preparing for battle heeds that advice. A Navy flier with whom I taught at the academy once told me that before he went on a mission, he took control of his emotions by uttering the mantra "compartmentalize, compartmentalize, compartmentalize." The trick, of course, is to know when to compartmentalize and when not to. Mission-preparedness seems to require it. But full Stoic detachment from emotions that record connection as well as loss can be too high a price to pay, even for the warrior. In particular, the capacity to grieve, to mourn one's dead, is crucial for warrior survival. Consider Coriolanus, the legendary fifth-century B.C. warrior who turns against his native city for banishing him. He is portrayed by Shakespeare as the paragon Stoic warrior. Physically strong and detached, more at home in the battlefield than with his wife and son, he is the military man par excellence. Fearless, he sheds few tears. And yet the play's turning point comes when Coriolanus remembers how to weep. "It is no little thing," he concedes, "to make mine eyes to sweat compassion." It is Coriolanus's mother, Volumnia, who reawakens his soul. Her entreaties persuade him to quit his siege of Rome and to restore peace. In weeping, Coriolanus finds human dignity.

Coriolanus may be a loner, a mama's boy at heart, touched only by a mother's tears. But for most soldiers, combat itself nurtures a camaraderie akin to the family relationships of childhood. The friendship of Achilles and Patroclus, central to the *Iliad*, symbolizes brothers-in-arms for all time. We can't begin to understand Achilles' near suicidal mourning for Patroclus without appreciating the sheer intensity of that bond. Moreover, we're misled if we think, as many readers have, that a friendship so passionate must be sexual, that only warrior-lovers could grieve as Achilles does for Patroclus.[3] Whether sexual partners or not, Achilles' grief for Patroclus could not be greater. The *Iliad*, like much of Greek culture, celebrates *philia*, the bond of friendship, with all its passion and shared journeys and recognizes the dignity of grief that comes when death or separation breaks the bond.

3. For a good discussion of this, see Jonathan Shay, *Achilles in Vietnam* (New York: Simon & Schuster, 1994).

In contemporary war, too, where soldiers put themselves at risk to defend each other, where Marines risk the living to save the dead or those with little breath left, the camaraderie of brothers- and sisters-in-arms tempers the sacrifices. Contemporary combat soldiers don't always have time to grieve. In missions where combat rarely stops, where pilots catapult from carriers only seconds after learning that the sorties before them will never return, where veterans come home in ones and twos aboard commercial airlines (as they did from Vietnam) and not en masse with their cohorts (as my father did from World War II aboard the converted Queen Mary), there is little time or place to sweat tears of compassion, yet deferring grief has devastating psychological costs.

The issues are raised penetratingly by Jonathan Shay in *Achilles in Vietnam*. As a Vietnam veterans' psychiatrist, he urges that communal grief work must again take place, as it did in the ancient world of the *Iliad*, if we are to help soldiers avoid the living death of postcombat trauma. Many of his patients say, "I died in Vietnam." Like Achilles at the death of Patroclus, they view themselves as already dead, dead and deadened by losing a close friend, "another self," as Aristotle would say.

Of course, the orthodox Stoic might say loss is not real loss if it falls outside what we can control through our own effort and virtue. We'd do better to change our habits of attachment than to pamper those whose false attachments create their losses. But we can learn from Stoicism without embracing its strict letter. What we can learn is that in the midst of our grieving, we still have a home in the world, connected to others whose fellowship and empathy support us, that we have inner resources that allow us to stand again after we have fallen. This human side of Stoicism can toughen us without robbing us of our humanity. I am reminded here of a stony-faced Marine colonel, who confided in me one evening that his most wrenching experience in war came not on the battlefield but in leaving behind his firstborn, a one-and-a-half-year-old boy. Going down to the plane, to begin his unaccompanied mission, his guts seized up on him. "I literally became sick to my stomach and vomited the whole way. I was violently ill the whole flight."

Another colleague told me that flying planes was easy. He said he was even amazed that he was paid to do what he loved. What was agony was leaving his wife and child behind. Nothing made that easier. Nothing could. These are tough warriors, Stoic warriors, but they are made of human stuff. They sweat tears of compassion. They heave their guts out when they leave their loved ones.

Other traditions, before and after Stoicism, present a philosophy with softer, human lines from the start. So Aristotle emphasizes throughout his ethical and political writings that the attachments of friendship are an irreducible part of a good life, and to lose a beloved friend is to lose part of what counts for happiness. One's own goodness cannot make up the difference, but necessarily relies on the goodness of others for completion. Similarly, Judeo-Christian traditions emphasize the healing power of love and compassion. In Exodus 15.26, God is portrayed as fearful and awesome, but also for the first time in the biblical narrative as a healer, ready to protect the Israelites against disease and provide them with water and bread in their forty-days-and-forty-nights trek through the wilderness.

The Stoics may struggle to capture the full palette of emotional attachment, but they profoundly recognize our cosmopolitan status in the world and stress, in a way significant for military education, the respect and empathy required of citizens of the world. Seneca in *On Anger* reminds his interlocutor, Novatus, that he is a citizen, not just of his country, but of that greater city of his, that universal commonwealth of the cosmos.[4] Each of us is a world citizen, the Stoics emphasize, following Diogenes the Cynic's notion of the human as a *kosmopolitês*, literally, "cosmic, universal citizen."[5] We are each parts of an extended

4. Seneca, "On Anger," II.31, in *Seneca: Moral and Political Essays*, John M. Cooper and J. F. Procop, eds. (Cambridge: Cambridge University Press, 1995).

5. As noted in Diogenes Laertius, *Lives of Eminent Philosophers*, R. D. Hicks, trans. (Cambridge, Mass.: Harvard University Press, 1972): 6.63. See also Epictetus, *Discourses*, W. A. Oldfather, trans. (Cambridge, Mass.: Harvard University Press, 1925): 2.10.3, I.9.2.

commonwealth and risk our individual integrity when we sever ourselves from the fellowship of that community. Marcus Aurelius makes the point graphically in terms of a much-used Stoic metaphor of the organic body:

> If you have ever seen a dismembered hand or foot or head cut off, lying somewhere apart from the rest of the trunk, you have an image of what a man makes of himself . . . when he . . . cuts himself off and does some unneighborly act . . . For you came into the world as a part and you have cut yourself off.[6]

Thus, on the Stoic view, it is as if we mutilate ourselves when we cut ourselves off from the global community. The notion of extended world citizenship became relevant to my Navy students as they prepared to risk their lives in foreign corners of the world and serve in multinational coalitions. Many students actively wrestled with what they saw as competing views of allegiance—to one's country and its leaders and to one's allies and their leaders. I recall one student who questioned whether he was really obligated to take orders from foreign commanders who might head integrated units to which he found himself assigned. His ultimate loyalty, he insisted, was to the Constitution of the United States, and after that, through a chain of command from the commander-in-chief to American commanders. In swearing to uphold the American Constitution he had not explicitly sworn to serve NATO or other international coalitions or agreements. This student wasn't alone in his skepticism. Many midshipmen, on their initiation day as plebes, have only the faintest idea that in swearing to uphold the Constitution they are pledging to a broader kind of world citizenship. The most compelling rebuttal to their skepticism often came from officers at the Academy who had themselves served in foreign coalitions as part of their military duty in the Persian Gulf and Bosnia. Many were engaged in training other nationals for more cohesive membership in coalitions.

6. Marcus Aurelius, *Meditations*, A. S. L. Farquharson, trans. (Oxford: Oxford University Press, 1989): 8.34.

Most understood implicitly that patriotism to country is not undermined by broader community allegiances. One can be fervently loyal to country and still serve under or command foreign officers who are part of broader international coalitions. Marcus Aurelius commanding troops and writing his memoirs today would most likely guard against a patriotism that demands narrow nationalism. For a nation and its military to sever itself from the larger alliance of nations would be an act of self-mutilation, a dismemberment of hand or foot from the whole body.

The Stoic Hierocles, writing in the first century A.D., adverts to the notion of cosmopolitanism as follows: "Each one of us [is] entirely encompassed by many circles, some smaller, others larger . . . The first circle contains parents, siblings, wife, and children." As we move outward, we move through grandparents, to neighbors, to fellow tribesmen and citizens, and ultimately to the whole human race. He insists that it is incumbent upon each of us "to draw the circles together somehow towards the center," to respect people from the outer circles as though they were from the inner. We are to do this "by zealously transferring those from the enclosing circles to the enclosed ones," to bring what is far to what is near, "to reduce the distance of the relationship with each person."[7]

Hierocles himself neither tells us exactly how we are to psychologically assimilate those in outer circles with inner ones so that we can come to identify with their circumstances, nor does he explore the nature of our duties, military or otherwise, in terms of which we show respect for others as we move outward in those circles. Later philosophers, themselves influenced by the Stoics, fill in the psychological story. We can do no better than turn to Adam Smith, the eighteenth-century Scottish Enlightenment writer. Sympathy, Smith argues, is a cognitive transport, a cognitive moment of becoming another. In his apt words, it involves "trading places in fancy," requiring an active

7. See A. A. Long and D. N. Sedley, *The Hellenistic Philosophers, Vol. 1* (Cambridge: Cambridge University Press, 1987): 349.

transference of the mind onto another, a simulation or role-play of what it is like to be another in his or her circumstances. "To beat time" to another's breast, he says, requires a projective capacity by which we imagine another's case:

> As we have no immediate experience of what other men feel, we can form no idea of the manner in which they are affected, but by conceiving of what we ourselves should feel in the like situation. Though our brother is upon the rack, as long as we ourselves are at our ease our senses will never inform us of what he suffers. They never did, and never can, carry us beyond our own person, and it is by the imagination only that we can form any conception of what are his sensations. . . . It is the impressions of our own senses only, not those of his, which our imaginations copy. By the imagination we place ourselves in his situation, we conceive ourselves enduring all the same torments, we enter, as it were, into his body and become in some measure the same person with him; and thence form some idea of his sensations, and even feel something which, though weaker in degree, is not altogether unlike them.[8]

The description brilliantly presages what contemporary philosophers of mind and cognitive psychologists now refer to as a "simulation" process by which we come to identify with others and, in some sense, "read" their minds. But again, we do well if we not only go forward in time, but backward. Smith was an avid reader of Cicero (as were most philosophers of the enlightenment period), and the notion of "placing ourselves in another's situation" becomes far clearer if we bring to bear Cicero's notion, in *On Duties*, of the different personae we wear.[9] To read another's mind one must "recenter" oneself on another, by imagining, as Cicero would put it, the shared personae we all have as rational

8. Adam Smith, *The Theory of Moral Sentiments* (Indianapolis: Liberty Classics, 1976 [1759]): 47–48.

9. M. T. Griffin and E. M. Atkins, eds. *On Duties* (Cambridge, Cambridge University Press, 1991): I.96ff. For a very helpful commentary, see Christopher Gill, "Personhood and Personality: The Four-*Personae* Theory in Cicero, *De Officiis* I" in *Oxford Studies in Ancient Philosophy, Vol. VI* (Oxford: Oxford University Press, 1988).

human beings, but also the personae we wear that are different from person to person. To empathize with or simply understand others, we must imagine what it is like to be another with distinctive temperaments and talents, in another's situation and circumstances, living life with life choices. It is not just that we "change" circumstances; we also change who we are in those circumstances. Thus, we don't simply put ourselves in others' shoes. We imagine ourselves *as others in their own shoes*. Sometimes we do this almost unconsciously. But at other times, as Hierocles says, we must keep zealously working at the transference.

We don't tend to think of the contemporary warrior as a "cosmopolitan" of this sort, but this is a central part of ancient Stoic teaching, and one that current-day warriors need to embrace as they increasingly face the demands of international coalitions and long-term peacekeeping missions in foreign countries. It is a notion we all need to take to heart as the demands of global citizenship become more and more a reality.

Sound Bodies and Sound Minds

Stoicism within the military revives another ancient Greek educational theme—the belief that strong bodies and minds must be cultivated together. Even in leg irons, with a broken leg and in solitary prison, Jim Stockdale forced himself to do more than a hundred sit-ups each morning. Controlling his own body, in the face of relentless torture and deprivation, was his way of staying alive and sane. He lived and breathed the Stoic doctrine that effort, endurance, and inner virtue are major components of human goodness. Self-endurance began with gaining control back of his own body, even in shackles.

For a public obsessed with consumption and consumer products, hungry for epicurean novelties but tired of pleats of adipose, the stripped-down life of military endurance and discipline offers an attractive tonic. Whether at eighteen or fifty, the military officer makes physical discipline part of the daily regimen. It shows up in the unmistakable, steel-gripped handshake, in workout regimens that begin or end each day, in physical training tests and weigh-ins that are part of a military record. All of my students participated in sports at the end of each class day, and most had additional workout regimens. The retired officers I worked with closely kept up their training, sporting youthful bodies well into their late sixties. My office suite mate, retired Adm. "Bud" Edney, a former pilot and commander in chief (CINC) of the North Atlantic region, became an avid spinner with his wife in his retirement years, and kept up with his biking and skiing as family activities. Adm. Larson, the four-star superintendent of the Naval Academy during my term, had a workout schedule in his home that began each day before 6 A.M. Others, who were once submariners and consigned to a treadmill on board, vowed now only to run outdoors, however inclement the weather.

For the military, strong bodies are mission-critical. The military trains warriors to have the strength to endure on the battlefield and the stamina to test human limits. Marine boot camp epitomizes the goal. The eleven-week moral and physical training culminates with what is called the crucible, two days of sleep and food deprivation, followed by an obstacle course in grueling environmental conditions. Survival is group survival. The goal is for the team to return as a team, even if it means coming home on the back of another.

As civilians, how should we view physical fitness when strong bodies are not exactly mission-critical, when there aren't jungles to pass through, daily thirty-mile hikes to endure, ammunition, persons, and bodies to carry to safety? In most white-collar professions, fit bodies are simply not part of the job description—legs of steel and arms of iron are neither here nor there. True, how we look in our clothes might subtly matter for job success, but there is nothing like the ubiquitous (if unwritten) military requirement to look good in a uniform.

This misses the obvious point. Civilian fitness *is* mission-critical in the very sense that any sort of healthy living requires it. Current worries about the significant rise of child and adult obesity are not misplaced. We need weight that doesn't overly tax vital organs, a strong heart to pump enough oxygen, adequate release of endorphins, serotonin, and other hormones to give us vitality and zest, bones that are dense enough to bear our own weight, and so on.

Ancient Greek and Roman thought is again an important source of guidance. For Plato and Aristotle, the great Greek philosophers who preceded the Stoics, virtue is as much a disposition toward self as toward others, and care of self includes how we care for our bodies. Temperance, for Aristotle, is a kind of internalized control in which we no longer have excessive bodily appetites and can moderate ourselves without much internal conflict. In short, we master indulgence and its impulses—lose the temptation, as one might say, to do otherwise. The prior developmental step is *egkrateia*, self-control or continence. Here we master appetite, but not without active struggle and forbearance. When we lapse from either of these forms of control, we are *akratic*, literally lacking in control or weak-willed. Appetite gets the better of judgment when we know what is best, but act against our knowledge. We avert our eyes. At times, Aristotle (and before him, Socrates) suggests that weakness of will is a kind of ignorance.[10] But we do best to think of it as *motivated* ignorance. We are ignorant only in the sense that we don't want to be reminded of what we know to be best.

Plato's dialogue, *The Republic*, has long influenced Western culture in its advocacy of an early education that includes gymnastics as well as music. But Plato insists that in the best education "the exercises and toils of gymnastics" are not mere "means to muscle;"[11] like music, bodybuilding is a way of shaping the psyche as well. It is a way of building mental discipline and spiritedness, a way of storing the general habit and procedures of control in mind as well as in muscle memory. The lessons of athletics are wasted, Plato insists, if their point is only to make a body more chiseled or agile. I have heard similar remarks from college athletic coaches who encourage young people to go into sports, not

10. See his discussion in *Nicomachean Ethics, VII.3*, Davis Ross, trans. (Oxford: Oxford University Press, 1998): VII.3.

11. Plato's *Republic*, G. Grube, trans. (Indianapolis: Hackett, 1974): Book III.

simply to become athletes, but to become individuals who have internalized the rigors of discipline and self-control. As Cicero remarks, strength of soul resembles "the strength and sinews and effectiveness of the body."[12]

In the contemporary world of the military, temperance and bodily fitness are monitored by external judges who test and keep records, who have the power to remove a sailor or marine if there is a lapse. Some of that surveillance can be harsh and, at times, insensitive to personal and gender differences. Women's bodies, by nature more fat-rich than men's, pose difficult challenges for the military in measuring body fat. Shortly after I left the Naval Academy, a woman who was an exemplary student and recipient of a prestigious prize for an ethics essay was eventually dismissed from the Academy on the grounds that her body fat exceeded the appropriate standard for her height. Even if the charts are different for men and women, the danger in a male culture, especially one that so prizes uniformity and cohesion, is that women will be shoehorned into male molds. For years, the military struggled with what sort of physical fitness requirements to impose on women, given women's different centers of gravity and strength. Standards now in place reflect reasonable gender differences, but resentment still lingers among some men that women are getting off the hook too easily. The reply to these complaints, as one of my colleagues at the Naval Academy once said, is easy. Ask the guy who objects to the women's standards if he would like his acceptable weight range pegged to the *women's* charts. Silence usually ensues.

In the civilian world, physical fitness and bodily health are more a matter of private virtue. Doctors have always taken records of weight and height and, in recent years, increasingly discuss smoking, diet, exercise, and alcohol consumption with patients. Their influence is typically at the level of recommendation rather than requirement. By

12. J. E. King, trans., *Tusculan Disputations* (Cambridge, Mass.: Harvard University Press, 1927): IV.13.30.

and large, the disciplined care of one's body sits squarely on one's own shoulders. Like most provinces of morality that fall outside legal purview, it is one's own business. This is as it should be. And yet with one out of two Americans overweight, the virtue of temperance seems to have become a personal virtue that is viewed as optional. "Self-indulgence is a human condition," Seneca writes, "even if in some pleasures wild animals are more intemperate than humans."[13] As with most virtues, temperance corrects a standing human condition, in this case, the tendency toward excessive appetite on the one hand, or bodily neglect on the other. We might add, temperance also corrects overcontrol.

If the Stoics are to offer inspiration, then the lesson to celebrate is not human control in excess, but in moderation. The Stoics constantly remind us how and in what way we have more dominion than we might at first think, whether it be in the physical sphere, moral, or emotional arena. But no plausible Stoicism can urge that we have unlimited dominion, even over our own virtue.

Good Manners, Good Morals

Strong characters and bodies are part of the military appeal, but so are manners. For those who believe manners build morals, the military offers the lesson in spades. At the mealtime formation at the Academy, visitors line up daily to see a brigade of crisply pressed uniforms and taut, straight bodies. Officers and midshipmen generally greet civilians with a "sir" or "ma'am," locked eye gaze, and firm handshake. They are helpful and courteous, polite and civil. The question that came to nag me as an ethicist was "how deep does surface conduct go?" Do manners lead to morals, etiquette to ethics? Should the civilian world, baffled by the degeneration of civility in public life, take better notice of the role of decorum in military culture? Is good conduct a part of good char-

13. J. M. Cooper and J. F. Procop, eds., "On Anger" in *Seneca: Moral and Political Essays* (Cambridge: Cambridge University Press, 1995): I.3.

acter? It is easy to be skeptical here. Codes of conduct are highly local. What one group finds a pleasing sign of respect, another may find overly formal or off-putting. Given the variability of conduct codes across cultures, how can behavior that is so culture-specific get to the heart of what matters morally? Moreover, much military conduct is mindless drill and compliance motivated by fear of those higher up in the chain of command. Can motivation so pegged to punishment still help an individual achieve inner virtue?

These legitimate concerns are not easily dismissed. They are criticisms most civilians would bring to a military environment, myself included. Yet I have become persuaded that the military is right in thinking that manners matter. Like moral acts such as helping or rescuing, showing courage or generosity, moral manners are also ways we routinely express our concern or respect for others. To look another in the eye but not stare them down, to listen without interrupting, to be mindful of what would offend, insult, or shame are in many cultures simply ways to acknowledge others as worthy of respect. True, certain manners may have more local coinage than others, but the fact that codes of etiquette vary culturally and that some codes are morally problematic does not generally impugn the connection of a good code of etiquette with morality.[14]

Stoic teachings are again instructive here. Seneca writes a lengthy, seven-book treatise on the subject of how to give and receive favors. It is a subject we might think, at first blush, befitting only the interests of Miss Manners and her readership. But as we read "On Favours," Seneca shows us how the matter is central to morality and crucial for human fellowship. Even a Stoic, bent on hardscrabble integrity and self-reliance, has an obligation to give and take gifts with grace: "When we have decided to accept [a gift], we should do so cheerfully. We should express our delight and make it obvious to our benefactor. We must show our

14. For a lively discussion, see Sarah Buss, "Appearing Respectful: The Moral Significance of Etiquette," in *Philosophy and Public Affairs* (1999).

gratitude by pouring out our feelings and bearing witness to them, not only in his presence but everywhere."[15] These attitudes are part of how we care for others and show our gratitude when cared for. Similarly, in *On Duties*, Cicero limns in considerable detail how "our standing, our walking, our sitting and our reclining, our countenances, our eyes and the movements of our hands" all are the outward expressions of our character.[16] Moreover, the Stoics hold that moral virtue requires a progression that moves from doing actions because they are appropriate and externally in accord with rules of right action, to doing actions that are right because they are motivated by virtue itself. What is mere good conduct in one person can in another be a morally worthy action because of its motivation.

Even if we grant the contribution of good manners to good morals, we might still doubt whether the military is the right model to watch. Consider Robert Duvall, playing the role of career officer in the movie *The Great Santini*. He painfully discovers that he can be the military colonel at home to his wife and children only at risk of losing them. He takes the gamble, for he knows no other way of winning respect. (Similarly, one midshipman told me after returning from Thanksgiving break that he was confused at home as to how to address his parents. Should he call them, "Sir" or "Ma'am" as he does his commanding officers, or just "Mom" and Dad" as he always has? The appropriate forms of respect had become fuzzy in his mind.)

Santini's notion of respect is based on hierarchy and rank as captured by the idea that a military person salutes the uniform, not the person, and the uniform higher up in the chain of command. (The sight is a common one at the Naval Academy as students with almost mechanically hinged forearms salute officers whom they pass in the

15. J. M. Cooper and J. F. Procop, eds. "On Favours" in *Seneca: Moral and Political Essays* (Cambridge, Cambridge University Press, 1995): II.22.

16. M. T. Griffin and E. M. Atkins, eds. "On Duties" using *Cicero: On Duties* (Cambridge: Cambridge University Press, 1991): I.128.

yard.) Outside the military, respect is a more democratic notion. Parents and elders may deserve special honor, but all, simply as persons, are worthy of basic respect. Moreover, respect in the civilian world is often conveyed in caring about the feelings of others, that one not shame, humiliate, or slight insofar as such attitudes offend a person's dignity. This is certainly an underlying theme in Seneca's treatise, "On Favours," but it is the rare commander who is terribly worried about the nuances of hurt feelings or squashed egos. Most officers would contend that a goodly amount of ego deflation is requisite for strong unit cohesion and achievement of the mission. Finally, there's the nagging issue of appearance, so critical to the military. *Appearing* respectful matters. Yet, why put so much emphasis on the pretense and artifice of behavior? Why reward the person who may be only a hypocrite or dissembler? Moreover, how does a straight back or hair pinned impeccably in place actually reflect on the goodness of a soul? In the ladies' room at the Academy, I saw women fix each strand of hair in place with bobby pins and spray so that not a wisp fell below regulation shoulder length. They clearly cared about the well-groomed look of an officer.

What underlies such care for decorum other than the desire to please? Both Cicero and Seneca argue that much decorum is underpinned by a desire to please and to take others' opinions into account.[17] They don't explicitly defend the stance, but imply that some degree of concern for how one is viewed is intimately connected with respect for others. Desiring to be agreeable, not to offend or disdain, not to slight, is part of what is involved in taking another seriously. We oughtn't make ourselves servile in the task or violate our own views of what is morally right in order not to offend. In cases where there is no conflict, concern for another at the level of emotional and formal comportment seems a part of moral respect for them. For this reason manners matter.

Even Immanuel Kant, the eighteenth-century German Enlightenment philosopher, notorious for his austere Stoic-inspired philosophy

17. See for example, Seneca, "On Favours," II.1–2, II.13; "On Duties," I.93–124.

of duty, urges that duty is not just inner virtue but a matter of manner and affect as well:

> No matter how insignificant these laws of refined humanity may seem, especially in comparison with pure moral laws, anything that promotes sociability, even if it consists only in pleasing maxims or manners, is a garment that dresses virtue to advantage, a garment to be recommended to virtue in more serious respects too.[18]

Controlling Anger and Rage

It is often said that anger is the underbelly of courage, that it mobilizes us to fight, that we need to keep the flame of anger kindled to be warriors. Cicero rehearses the view: "no stern commands" can rally ourselves or others, whether on the battlefield or off, "without something of the keen edge of irascibility." Irascibility is "the whetstone of bravery."[19] Both Cicero and Seneca deny the claim. Indeed, the Stoics argue strenuously that anger and rage are pernicious emotions that do more damage than good. "No plague has cost the human race more," Seneca says in his famous treatise, "On Anger." A true Stoic warrior doesn't rely on anger to fight his battles.

Part of the problem with anger, according to the Stoics, is that it can't easily be moderated—once turned on, it can't easily be turned off. It is a runaway passion, the Stoics say, whose stride outpaces the command of reason. It is "the most rabid and unbridled of all emotions,"[20] says Seneca. It perverts the body and mind, and literally disfigures the face. Seneca is graphic in his portrait. Those who are angry have

> eyes ablaze and glittering, a deep flush over all the face as blood boils up from the vitals, quivering lips, teeth pressed together, bristling hair

18. *Anthropology from a Pragmatic Point of View*, Mary J. Gregor, trans. (The Hague: Nijoff, 1974): 282.
19. See *Tusculan Disputations* IV.19.21.
20. See "On Anger," III.16.

> standing on end, breath drawn in and hissing, the crackle of writhing limbs, groans and bellowing. . . . the hideous horrifying face of swollen self-degradation—you would hardly know whether to call the vice hateful or ugly.[21]

Seneca insists that we can control this hideous frenzy and rid ourselves of its corrosive effects by a bold straightforward method: let go of the kinds of attachments to honor or reputation, or victory or wealth, which when threatened make us angry. These are not real goods, he teaches, following ancient Stoic doctrine. True, the Stoics concede, they are the kinds of goods that we might like to have and that we prefer rather than not prefer, but having them adds nothing substantive to our happiness. They are not genuine parts of happiness which in the Stoic view (which closely follows Socrates' teachings) is only a function of inner virtue. Its prosperity is the prosperity of virtue, not of wealth, fortune, or the opinions of others.

The full Stoic view may be hard to swallow. We do depend on others' opinions of us, and think our reputation in a community matters. We would be different creatures, far less social and communal, far less able to achieve the very *Stoic* goals of community and fellowship, if we were indifferent to others' praise and blame, compliments or slights. We couldn't raise children without praise and blame from parents. Yet, in holding that certain emotions, like anger, involve mistaken values, the Stoics presuppose something more fundamental and more revealing, namely, that emotions are themselves evaluations or appraisals, ways of judging the world. Aristotle holds that emotions involve construals about the world, though on his position those construals are neither systematically false nor misleading.[22] They are part and parcel of knowing the world accurately and wisely—a view that has been reappropriated by contemporary cognitive psychologists. In that view, emotions involve cognitive assessments of the environment that lead to

21. Ibid., 1.2.
22. See, for example, the account of emotions in *Rhetoric* II.

arousal and desiderative responses. So sadness involves an appraisal that I have been hurt, love the idea that he is attractive, or pity the thought that someone has suffered unjustly. The Stoics go whole hog, though, in holding that emotions are nothing but beliefs, and consequently, that we can change emotions in their entirety by changing beliefs. There is no remainder. We might say they are the first to advocate a thorough-going cognitive therapy as a method of emotional change. Under their aegis, the particular form that cognitive therapy takes is philosophical dialectic. "Row the oars of dialectic," Cicero says, if you are to transform the soul.[23]

Few of us hold with the Stoics that emotions are nothing but beliefs or as corrigible as them. Nor are we likely to endorse the Stoic doctrine that the kind of beliefs emotions involve predominantly embody false values. Rather, most of us probably think, with Aristotle and current cognitive psychologists, that emotions often give us truthful views of the world, even if sometimes exaggerated or magnified. We also tend to think that the desires that lace emotions and the physiological arousals expressive of emotions make for states that are as much body as mind and hence hard to relinquish by a sheer act of will. Few of us are ready to embrace wholeheartedly the Stoic doctrine that all goods other than the pure goodness of our souls ought to be matters of complete indifference to us, things from which we can fully detach in a search for a meaningful life. Yet despite the harshness of some of their views, the Stoics propound a view that we are likely to have considerable sympathy with, and this is that to some degree, emotions embody ways of thinking about the world and evaluating it. Emotions judge the world, and when we subtly shift those ways of thinking (i.e., stop thinking that something is an offense, loss, injury, or attraction), we shift our emotional states. What most of us probably dispute is that the cognitive shift is itself sufficient for an emotional shift, that feeling can be reduced to believing.

23. Cicero, *Tusculan Disputations*, J. E. King, trans. (Cambridge, Mass.: Harvard University Press, 1945).

We now need to return to the original specific Stoic claim that anger is an emotion needing extirpation. Can a Stoic, who roots out all anger, be trained to kill? Does this feature of a Stoic education make sense for a military person? I would suggest the harder conceptual problem is not in considering the possibility that a warrior lacks anger, but that a virtuous person is devoid of all anger. To be a soldier, defending principle, abiding by rules of engagement, cognizant of the constraints of just war and just conduct in war embodied in such documents as the Law of Land warfare or the Geneva Conventions, in fact, requires a principled response to the demands of warfare. To act out of frenzy or rage, to systematically dehumanize the enemy in the way that anger toward an enemy often requires, for a commander to incite his troops by bloody thirst for revenge, for a pilot to be battle-happy in a way that makes him nonchalant about the no-fly zone, is to risk running afoul of the moral framework of war. No one can fight without the adrenaline rush of aggression and competitive spirit, and it is a drill sergeant's job to push his troops to know those emotions well. But that physiological arousal may not itself be underpinned by the kinds of judgments that Seneca claims underlie irascibility and rage.

Even if we can conceive of a warrior who fights best because of principle rather than anger, can we conceive of a virtuous person who leaves behind his senses of anger, moral indignation, and outrage? Consider retired Chief Warrant Officer Hugh Thompson, the man some have called the hero of My Lai.[24] On March 16, 1968, he was flying his observation helicopter when he spotted several wounded people on the ground and a dike where a group of GIs approached an injured, unarmed woman of about twenty. Later one officer prodded the woman with his foot, then killed her. Minutes later Thompson saw dozens of bodies in an irrigation ditch, their writhing movements suggesting that some were still alive. American infantrymen beside the

24. For my account, I have drawn on the report by Michael Hilton and Kevin Sim in their *Four Hours in My Lai* (New York: Penguin, 1992).

ditch were taking a cigarette break from battle, taking off their steel helmets for a moment of respite. Several minutes later, he saw one of the sergeants shooting at people in the ditch and his worst fears were confirmed. With his side gunner, Larry Colburn, and his crew chief, Glenn Andreotta, Thompson landed the helicopter, telling Colburn to "open up " on the GI's—"open up on 'em, blow 'em away"—if they opened fire at him as he intervened.

After some thirty years of silence, the Army belatedly decorated Hugh Thompson with the prestigious Soldier's Medal for his valor on that day in My Lai. Shortly after, he visited Annapolis for a public address, and we spent some time talking together. What were those moments of sighting the massacre at My Lai like, I asked. What did he feel? In carefully chosen words, he remembered thinking that what he witnessed was much like Nazi behavior during the Holocaust. At the time, he thought American soldiers didn't behave that way. They didn't commit genocide. He had shared similar thoughts with the midshipmen that day, and the traces of anger and disbelief were still visible in his face and audible in his voice as he recalled approaching the GIs wielding weapons against innocents. He himself didn't use the words "moral outrage," but it was clear that his judgments about the horrors he saw that day were the judgments that constitute moral anger. Thirty years later, upon returning to the village of My Lai for a memorial, he was met by one of the village women who survived the slayings. He remembered her then as a young mother. She was now a frail, aging woman. She yanked at Thompson's sleeve and implored, "Why did the American GI's kill my family? Why? Why were they different from you?" He broke down in tears and said, "I don't know. I don't know. That is not how I was taught to behave."[25]

If we follow Seneca, do we support an education that would have forced Thompson to look on with dispassionate disinterest, a kind of

25. I am remembering the gist of the conversation as it appeared on CBS's *60 Minutes*.

Stoic apathy, that could incite neither rage nor grief? Would we root out the core of Thompson's virtue and humanity? Seneca himself is inconsistent on the point. Anger is the clear enemy in his essay, yet he closes his piece with the following exhortation, "While we still draw breath, while we still remain among human beings, let us cultivate our humanity."[26] A Stoicism committed to the cultivation of humanity and human fellowship cannot, in fact, eliminate all human anger. As frenzied and blinding as anger's outbursts are, as dehumanizing as rage can be, anger expressed in the right way at the right time is the sure sign of humanity. Aristotle, not the Stoics, got this point right: anger can be morally fine and praiseworthy. If the Stoics improve upon Aristotle it is in reminding us that emotions are, more often than we think, a matter of our responsibility. The Stoics urge that the emotions are volitional states. We are not just *affected* when we suffer emotions, but as the Stoics put it, we *yield* or *give assent* to certain judgments implicit in those emotions.[27] Even if we reluctantly embrace a notion of emotions as voluntary, it is undeniable that over time we have considerable dominion over how we respond emotionally. We take charge of how we cultivate our humanity, including, I would add, our anger.

Conclusion

The Stoics offer important lessons for the military, and, I would urge, for civilians as well. They give guidance in shaping a character education that takes seriously the values of discipline and self-mastery, while recognizing our dependence upon others not only in small communities, but also globally. We have seen that Stoic lessons of self-sufficiency and self-mastery are crucial antidotes to the indulgences of consumer-

26. "On Anger," III.43. For an insightful discussion of "On Anger," see Martha Nussbaum, *The Therapy of Desire* (Princeton University Press, 1994): Chapters 10 and 11.

27. For a nuanced description of the voluntary and involuntary aspects of emotional experience, see Seneca's "On Anger," II.1–4.

ism and appetite that plague the contemporary scene. The point is not to idealize the life of deprivation or slavery (as a Stoic like Epictetus may seem sometimes to do), but rather to cultivate the inner resources and virtues that allow for a measure of control in the face of strong temptations and hard losses. The Stoic wisdom is that we have dominion in more areas of our lives than we acknowledge. Our physical strength can be built, our emotions affect us, but we also regulate them and learn habits of mind and expression that convey our cares.

The Stoics make the latter point by suggesting that proper emotions are forms of judgment that we openly accept and willfully allow. In the case of an emotion like anger, they say we can control the judgments we consent to and endorse. We have seen how this stance has both attractions and dangers. We know without being card-carrying Stoics that reflection allows us to revise overly hasty views about what may annoy, insult, or offend, and that these revised judgments help us to change how we feel, in some cases releasing us from the grip of unreasonable anger. The Stoics, however, insist that all anger is poisoned and that the truly virtuous person is rid entirely of its venom, but we have argued against this extreme view. Anger can also show its face as moral outrage, indignation, and a sense of injustice. There are human moments when anger is precisely the right response, however much we may lose ourselves in the reaction. Similarly it is so for grief, compassion, and love. Perhaps the Stoic lesson is that there are ways of *recovering* our mastery even after we have let go, forms of resilience and self-governance that allow for stability in the face of the strongest winds.

The Stoics also insist upon our cosmopolitan status as citizens of the universe, not isolated individuals or isolated nations. Military and civic education must emphasize not only loyalty to country, but also loyalty to values beyond national borders. My midshipmen needed reminders of their broader citizenship in the urgent circumstance of chain of command: from whom should they take orders? For many, the question of whom to respect, obey, and assist are more diffuse, but the young civilian, no less than the junior military officer, needs to know that moral obligations and wider circles of allegiance extend beyond national borders. It is not just our economy that is global, but in a pointed way, our moral community as well.

I have turned to the military as a case study for exploring Stoicism and have done so upon the military's own lead. Many Navy officers I have worked with have implicitly and explicitly embraced Stoicism for guidance. I argue that we have much to reap from the rich Stoic texts. But I also urge a critical attitude in the face of more orthodox Stoic tenets. The task as moral educators is to shape a Stoicism with a human face. As Coriolanus, Shakespeare's legendary Stoic warrior realized, "it is no little thing to make mine eyes to sweat compassion."

A Communitarian Position on Character Education

Amitai Etzioni

AMERICA'S MORAL AND social fabric is weakening. Too often we demand rights without assuming responsibilities, pursue entitlements while shying away from obligations. More broadly, as the increase in antisocial behavior over the last decades indicates, we have lost our commitment to values we all share and few new ones have arisen to replace those that were lost.

We should not treat violence, drug abuse, illegitimacy, promiscuity, abusive attitudes toward people of different backgrounds, alcoholism, poor academic performance, and other social maladies as isolated phenomena. They reflect several social factors, but key among them is weakness of character—the inability to resist temptation and adhere to prosocial values. Communitarians maintain that values do not fly on

This piece draws, to a limited extent, on Amitai Etzioni, *The Spirit of Community* (New York: Crown Publishers, Inc., 1993).

their own wings. To shore up our moral foundations we must pay attention to the social institutions that undergird our values. These include the family, schools, the community (including voluntary associations and places of worship), and society (as a community of communities).

The focus here is on one institution, the school. Given that roughly 88 percent of students still attend public schools, they are what this examination deals with. It is assumed that even if families—whose societal task is to introduce children to moral values and lay the foundation of their characters—work perfectly, schools still need to round off the task. Given the burden and challenges parents face, they are rarely able to perform their job fully and hence even more responsibility falls on schools. It follows that schools should make the development of good character one of their primary responsibilities.

Those who consider such a mission at the obvious center of education should note that for quite a few years pressure has been growing to dedicate ever more resources, energy, and time to teaching ever-younger children academics. Newly introduced tests, on academic subjects, and drives to teach preschool children to read, all add to the neglect of attention to character education in public schools.

Principles of Character Education: An Overview

Here are the high points:

1. Values education is a crucial part of public education that should be fostered in schools. There cannot be a value-free or value-neutral education. Schools must supplement the moral education provided at home, especially when homes are not intact.
2. Character-building is at the root of upholding values. Without *character* education, merely knowing what is right is no assurance that we will do it and incorporate these values into our

lives. Critical to developing character are the two capabilities of self-discipline and empathy. Self-discipline is required because without it individuals cannot control their impulses and will grow up to be uncivil, unethical, and ineffectual. External controls are needed up to a point but if extended beyond that point, they undermine the cultivation of self-discipline. Empathy, the capacity to walk in another person's shoes, is also essential. It is at the foundation of many values, and without it those who are self-disciplined might commit themselves to nefarious purposes.

3. Character education should imbue students with the full range of school experiences—the human curriculum as well as the academic curriculum. It should not be limited to classes on civics, nor is it only a matter of curriculum content. The way sports are conducted, grades are allotted, teachers behave, and corridors and parking lots are monitored all import moral messages and significantly affect character development.

The preceding observations inform the following specific comments.

Extracurricular activities, especially sports, should not be considered extra, but a vital part of education. We must strive to develop stronger ties between these activities and character development. Sport is important not merely for a healthy body and as a substitute for street activities, but also a way to learn to play by the rules, bond, develop camaraderie, and much more.

The ways schools deal with infractions is of special significance for character education. Schools that ignore petty violence, gross disorder in the corridors, cafeteria and parking areas, disrespect for the teacher and the facilities, are undermining character education. The same holds for schools that hand out rewards (especially grades) too easily, provide automatic promotion and graduation, and allot rewards on the basis of nonachievement-based considerations. Peer mentoring of students and patrols of shared spaces, guided by professionals, is a promising way to enhance character education.

Schools should teach those values shared by the community, such as veracity and treating others with dignity. The teaching of values particularly dear to the heart of subgroups should be reserved for religious and other private schools. The suggestion that there are only few such values, or that shared commitment to them holds only as long as they remain highly abstract, is not in line with the facts.

A public school should teach about the social role and historical significance of religion but not advocate a particular religion. One ought to support efforts such as those of the Williamsburg Charter to find common ground on religious issues that divide us and to find space in schools to discuss these issues.

"Value-free" sex education is unacceptable. Teaching family values without information about ways to prevent transmission of disease and unwanted pregnancies is dangerous. We need education for interpersonal relations, family life, and intimacy that provides a normative context for sex education and shares age-appropriate specific information on the subject. Students should learn about the value of delaying sexual involvement and the merits of abstinence while receiving contraception information to protect them and others if they do become sexually active. The second message need not cancel out the first one.

Schools within Communities

Schools are often expected to correct society's ills but the opposite must be considered. Schools need all the external help that can be marshaled to discharge their duties. Parents and other community members and institutions should see themselves as partners rather than as outsiders.

Parents should be deeply involved in all aspects of formulating and implementing school policies, curricula, discipline, community service and, above all, values issues. While teachers' and other educators' professional knowledge should be heeded, on matters of character the voice of parents and communities should take precedence, within constitutional limits as long as the policies favored do not pose a danger to life and limb. (For example, a school may well favor turning the school into a gun-free zone and oppose a community that favors allowing students to carry concealed weapons.)

One should support community schools that also serve as community centers. Schools should gradually shift to remain open more months a year, longer hours, and even during weekends. This cannot be done overnight, but the farmers' calendar is no longer useful.

Community service, when properly conducted, can be an effective means of developing civic commitments and skills by doing rather than by merely studying. Although community service should be the practicum for civics, imposing it on students defeats the purpose of developing the taste for volunteerism.

Greater integration must be achieved between work and schooling. Educators need to search for ways to connect schooling with activities that make sense to young people. Many businesses that employ high school students part-time ought to recognize that they are educators as well. These early work experiences will either reinforce responsible habits and attitudes or serve as lessons in poor civics and deficient work ethics. Corporations and small businesses should work with schools to better structure employment opportunities for adolescents to build character and prepare them for their futures.

Schools should be viewed as nascent communities. Students and teachers should have the same basic goals and should be discouraged from approaching one another in an adversarial or legalistic fashion. Although the basic rights of students must be fully respected, maintaining civility in schools should not require full court hearings and the cross-examination of witnesses when disciplining students. Simplified hearings, limited appeals, mediating, and similar measures are more appropriate for a school setting. We prefer that disruptive students receive more education rather than banishment. However, when these measures fail, schools should not be unduly hampered in removing those who destroy the learning environment.

Diversity within Unity

Enhanced diversity in the curricula and in the composition of the school enriches us, but also exposes us to the dangers of tribalism. Diversity should be advanced, but within the context of unity. We are richer if we learn about other cultures and traditions and develop more respect for others. But we must share certain basics, and above all, the superior value of the democratic form of government, the importance of the Constitution and its Bill of Rights, and the tolerance of one another. Educators should be mindful of the theme implied in the saying, "We all came on different ships but now we ride in the same boat."

No class should teach hate against another group. We all have troubling parts in our respective histories. We need to learn reconciliation without forgetting the lessons of the past, lest we repeat them.

Teaching new immigrant children in their native languages for a limited time may ease their transition, but we should avoid prolonged separation of education along ethnic or racial lines.

Discussion

Character development entails acquiring the capacity to control impulses and to mobilize for acts other than the satisfaction of one's self. Workers need such self-control so that they can stick to their tasks rather than saunter into work late and turn out slapdash products—so that they are able to observe a work routine that is often not very satisfying by itself. Citizens and community members need self-control so that they do not demand ever more services and handouts while being unwilling to pay taxes and make contributions to the common good. Self-control makes people more tolerant of others from different ethnic, racial, and political backgrounds. This tolerance is at the foundation of democratic societies.

Newborns have almost no capacity for impulse control or mobilization to tasks that require deferment of gratification; they are preoccupied with their immediate needs and desires. Education channels some of these drives to energize an internal regulator that gives self-direction to the person and is often referred to as character. Education ties gratification to the development of qualities that are socially useful and morally appropriate (a process psychologists call sublimation). By relating satisfaction to being punctual, completing a task, and taking other people's feelings into account, by playing by the rules, one acquires the ability to abide by moral tenets and to live up to social responsibilities.

It is possible to overeducate and to draw too much of the ego's energies into the inner mechanisms of self-control. This is what is meant by being "uptight"—people who are obsessed with their careers or achievements are unable to relax or show affection. Such excessive self-control has concerned social scientists in the past, especially in the sixties, and has led to a call for less character education in favor of more unbounded ego expression. Excessive self-control, however, is uncommon in contemporary America; indeed, many youngsters come to school with a grossly deficient capacity to guide themselves. The fact that a larger proportion of the young find it difficult to be punctual, get up in the morning, do homework on their own, and complete tasks in an orderly and timely fashion are but the most visible indications of a much deeper deficiency. As a result, schools must engage in character education. This is where various commissions that have studied educational deficits went wrong. By and large, they argue for loading students with more hours of science, foreign language, math, and other skills and bodies of knowledge. *But you cannot fill a vessel that has yet to be cast.* Character formation is an essential prerequisite—both so that pupils can learn, and so that by the time they graduate they will command the necessary human qualities to be effective, responsible adults.

Discipline, Self-Discipline, and Internalization

Parents and educators often stress the importance of discipline in character formation and in the moral education of the new generation of

Americans. In several public-opinion surveys, teachers, school administrators, and parents rank a lack of discipline as the number-one problem in our schools. They correctly perceive that in a classroom where students are restless, impatient, disorderly, and disrespectful, where rules and routines cannot be developed and maintained, learning is not possible.

So far, so good. Unfortunately, discipline, as many people understand it, takes on an authoritarian meaning. A well-disciplined environment is often considered one in which teachers and principals lay down the law and will brook no talking-back from students, who show respect by rising when the teacher enters the room and speak only when spoken to. In quite a few states physical punishment is still considered an effective way to maintain discipline. I maintain that if discipline is achieved by authoritarian means, youngsters will behave as long as they are closely supervised and fear punishment. But as soon as the authorities turn their backs, they tend to misbehave and their resentment at being coerced expresses itself in some form of antisocial behavior. This is because the discipline is linked to punishment rather than to a general sense of right and wrong.

What the pupil—and the future adult—requires is self-discipline, the inner ability to mobilize and commit to a task he or she believes in and to feel positive—that is, rewarded—for having done so. This quality is developed when the voice of authority is internalized and becomes part of the person's inner self, his ego. Internalization occurs in structured environments, but not under authoritarian conditions. What is not needed is close, continuous external supervision (and certainly not the kind of punitive environment that comes to mind when we think about military academies). Rather, what is required is a school structure made up of authority figures, rules, and organization of tasks that motivate students by providing clear guidelines. These must be both firmly upheld and be reasonable and justified, so that students can understand the need to abide by them.

Educational requirements must, in turn, be clearly stated, and the link between requirements and goals fully explained. Curricula should be neither arbitrary nor subject to the whim of an individual teacher. To foster self-discipline, assignments must be "do-able," appropriately checked, and properly rewarded. When they are excessive and mechanical (such as the time one of my high-school sons was required to memorize the names of all the Indian tribes that resided in America), or when rewards are allocated according to irrelevant criteria (such as teacher favoritism, minority status, or undue parental influence), requirements become dictates and not sources of involvement and ways to internalize commitments, to build self-discipline.

Character and Moral Education

Although character formation lays the psychic foundation both for the ability to mobilize to a task and to behave morally (by being able to control impulses and defer gratification), it is contentless: it does not educate one to a specific set of virtues or values. It provides the rectitude needed to tell the truth even if the consequences are unpleasant, but it does not teach the value of being truthful. It enables a person to refrain from imposing his sexual impulse on an unwilling partner, but it does not teach him that it is morally unacceptable to rape. Developing character without attention to value education is like trying to develop the muscles of an athlete without having a particular sport in mind. This statement inevitably raises the question: Whose values?

The challenge "Whose values will you teach?" is readily answered by starting with the many values that we all share (not only in one community or by Americans, but much more widely). Nobody considers it moral to abuse children, rape, steal, commit murder, be disrespectful of others, discriminate, and so on.

Some values, a small subset of the total in well-functioning communities, are contested. These exceptions can be dealt with either by letting the students learn about both sides of the issue or by openly omitting them. Moreover, these issues are helpful in showing the pain of moral conflicts and the merit of genuine consensus-building, a consensus we do have on most values. Sure, say the opponents, but people agree only on vague generalities that almost amount to banalities. They argue: When you come down to specifics, disagreements will dominate, and then whose specifics will you teach?

In response I note that first, we would be way ahead if we could get everyone to truly subscribe to all these values and only argue with one another over the specific applications. Second, when it comes to specifics, there is more consensus than at first seems to be the case. Professor William Damon points to the following conducts that deserve our attention:

> A counselor is calling a student's home about apparently excused absences, only to find that the parent's letters have been forged. A young boy is in the principal's office for threatening his teacher with a knife. Three students are separated from their class after hurling racial epithets at a fourth. A girl is complaining that her locker has been broken into and all her belongings stolen. A small group of boys are huddling in a corner, shielding an exchange of money for drug packets. In the playground, two girls grab a third and punch her in the stomach for flirting with the wrong boy. (Personal communication.)

Using these and other such behaviors as education opportunities is sure to keep teachers busy for years to come. This suggests that we have to attend to other sources of these behaviors—for instance, by rebuilding community within the adult world, which these children often emulate.

One need not worry that educators will brainwash students who are captive audiences in their classrooms and make them accept their moral viewpoints. Students are exposed to a large variety of voices, from television, magazines, porn shops, peers, and many others. There are natural checks and balances built into the social environment. If somewhere one teacher advanced a moral concept that was outside the community consensus, say, that we must all become vegetarians, pacifists, or Zen Buddhists, the students would have plenty of other sources to draw on to counter such teaching. Indeed, the opposite is true: if typical educators, whose values tend to be well within the community range, refrain from adding their moral voices to the cacophony of voices to which the students are exposed, the students would miss one perspective and remain exposed only to all the other voices, less committed to values the community holds dear.

The Import of Experiences

How does one teach moral values, as opposed to merely building up the capacity for moral reasoning and disputations? How does one build up moral commitments? One way far surpasses all others: experiences are more effective teachers than lectures and textbooks, although their narrative is also valuable. This is particularly evident in extracurricular activities, especially sports. True, these can be abused, such as when coaches focus on winning as the only object, and neglect to instill learning to play by the rules, teamwork, and camaraderie. Graduates of such activities tend to be people who are aggressive, maladjusted members of the community. However, if coaches and the messages they impart are well integrated into the values education of a school, and if parents see the importance of using sports to educate rather than to win, sports can be a most effective way to enhance values education.

Why do extracurricular activities command extraordinary power? Because they generate experiences that are effective educational tools. Thus, if one team plays as a bunch of individuals and loses because its adversary played as a well-functioning team, the losing players learn—in a way that no pep talk or slide show could teach them—the merit of playing as a team.

The same holds for other activities that take place at school. They provide experiences that have deep educational effects, either positive or negative. The first step toward enhancing the moral educational role of schools is to increase the awareness and analysis of the school as a set of experiences. Schools should be seen not as a collection of teachers, pupils, classrooms, and curricula. Instead, we need to include the parking lots: Are they places in which wild driving takes place and school authorities are not in sight, or places where one learns respect for others' safety, regulated either by faculty or fellow students? Are the cafeterias places where students belt each other with food and the noise is overwhelming, or civilized places where students have meaningful conversations over lunch? Are the corridors areas where muscles and stature are required if one is to avoid being pushed aside by bullies, or are they safe conduits patrolled by faculty or students? Does vandalism go unpunished, are drugs sold openly, and are pupils rewarded or punished according to criteria other than achievement (perhaps because they avoid confrontation, obey without question, or come from affluent or otherwise socially preferred backgrounds)? Is vandalism held in check (and when it does occur, the damage corrected by the offending students), drug sales swiftly and severely dealt with, and students treated under rational general criteria?

A powerful example of how one may generate experiences in a classroom is found in Iowa. It is a well-known case in point, but one that deserves to be recalled. In 1968, Jane Elliott, a third-grade teacher, concluded that instead of talking about the plight of black Americans shortly after the assassination of Martin Luther King, Jr., she would teach her third-graders about discrimination by affecting their experiences. Elliott divided her class into two groups by eye color—the blue- and brown-eyed. "Today," she said one Friday, "the blue-eyed people will be on the bottom and the brown-eyed people on the top." Elliott continued: "What I mean is that brown-eyed people are better than blue-eyed people. They are cleaner than blue-eyed people. They are more civilized than blue-eyed people. And they are smarter than blue-eyed people."

The experiment's effects were swift and severe. "Long before noon, I was sick," Elliott recalls. "I wished I had never started it . . . . By the lunch hour, there was no need to think before identifying a child as blue- or brown-eyed. I could tell simply by looking at them. The brown-eyed children were happy, alert, having the times of their lives. The blue-eyed children were miserable." The children had learned through experience what discrimination is like and were deeply affected by the exercise. Brown-eyed Debbie Anderson said: "I felt mad [on blue-eye-preferred Monday] . . . I felt dirty. And I did not feel as smart as I did on Friday." Student Theodore Perzynski wrote: "I do not like discrimination. It makes me sad. I would not like to be angry all my life."

A mother of one of Elliott's students said:

> I want you to know that you've made a tremendous difference in our lives since your Discrimination Day exercise. My mother-in-law stays with us a lot, and she frequently uses the word "nigger." The very first time she did it after your lesson, my daughter went up to her and said, "Grandma, we don't use that word in our house, and if you're going to say it, I'm going to leave until you go home." We were delighted. I've been wanting to say that to her for a long, long time. And it worked, too. She's stopped saying it.

Such an experience leaves a strong and lasting impression. In 1984, Jane Elliott's class had a reunion. Former student Susan Rolland reported: "I still find myself sometimes, when I see some blacks together and I see how they act, I think, well, that's black . . . . And then later, as I said, I won't even finish the thought before I remember back when I was in that position." Verla Buls added: "We was [sic] at a softball game a couple of weekends ago, and there was this black guy I know. We said, 'Hi,' and we hugged each other, and some people really looked, just like, 'What are you doing with him?' And you just get this burning feeling in you. You just want to let it out and put them through what we went through to find out they're not any different." Other students reported that their career choices were influenced by the discrimination experience. Several chose to join the Peace Corps or work with other cultures overseas.

Less Rotation, More Bonding

For teachers to be more than purveyors of information and skills, for them to be able to educate, to build character, they must bond more closely with students than they do now in many schools. Such bonding may be encouraged by arranging for less rotation of classes and pupils. Many American high schools were reorganized as if a powerful sociological engineer intent on minimizing the bonds between students and teachers sought to ensure that whatever peer bonds formed would not be classroom-based. These effects stem from the fact that students are reshuffled each time the bell rings, every forty-five minutes or so, while the various subject teachers stay put. Students, especially in larger schools, rarely develop bonds as members of a class group, because the class members they related to in one period are different from the ones they see in the next. Because of this, peer groups, which often hold sway over members, especially in moral matters, are not classroom-based and are formed for other reasons often irrelevant to education. Peer groups are likely to be formed around other occasions and values, whether it is racing cars or rock music. This makes it rather difficult for teachers to draw upon these peer bonds and challenge them to support moral education. Peer groups don't necessarily have to oppose community and educational values, but sociological studies show that they often do, and they rarely are mobilized by educators on the side of moral education in the typical high-rotation schools.

Another result is that teachers cannot form bonds with their students, because they hardly have an opportunity to know them. Teachers are typically responsible for a subject, and not for a class or a given group of pupils, for example, all those in the eleventh grade, section five. Thus, the highly specialized school organization is, in effect, a systematic hindrance to bonding with educators, which is an essential prerequisite for moral education.

High schools should be reorganized to facilitate experience-based moral education. Teachers should be in charge of a particular class, teaching the same group of youngsters, say, three subjects (especially those rich in value content such as history and literature), or two subjects and civics. The same teacher would also be the class's homeroom teacher, explicitly in charge of disciplinary matters. Discipline should be sought not as if the teacher were a punitive police officer, but a faculty member whose task it is to use instances of improper conduct to enhance moral education. Schools might also institute a policy whereby such teachers would follow the same students from ninth through twelfth grades.

Such changes would, in turn, necessitate changes in the ways the teachers themselves are trained, to make them less specialized. Many teachers, especially those who teach humanities or liberal arts, are already broadly grouped. In any event, without more bonding and contacts that are more encompassing, extensive, and value-laden, moral education is unlikely to succeed.

Building Democratic Community: A Radical Approach to Moral Education

F. Clark Power

SINCE 1975, I have worked with Lawrence Kohlberg and his colleagues to develop the Just Community approach to moral education. This approach focuses on building moral community through involving students in democratic decision-making. Although the Just Community approach embodies the highest ideals of our nation, our efforts to disseminate it have met with entrenched resistance. In spite of the approach's demonstrated effectiveness in promoting moral development, building cohesive community, fostering democratic skills, and reducing disciplinary problems, principals and teachers typically regard it as unrealistic. Although schools espouse democracy and community in their mottoes and mission statements, they are not democracies; principals and teachers govern autocratically. Few, if any, formal opportunities are available for students to participate in deciding what matters most to students—school discipline and social life. Although most schools have some form of student government, its function is typically and carefully confined to organizing social events and fund-raisers. Schools beyond the elementary level are not cohesive communities; cliques and crowds dominate the social landscape. Although most schools pay lip service to building community through sports programs and school assemblies, few establish a genuine sense of solidarity that cuts across sex, race, social class, and friendship group.

Although the character education movement has been growing rapidly in the United States, surprisingly little attention has been paid to the school environment. As I will argue, schools, particularly junior high and high schools, often undermine character education by fostering cultures inimical to the values taught in class. Principals and teachers simply fail to recognize how the culture co-opts their well-intentioned efforts to teach virtue. When we think of schools, we think of the curriculum, methods of teaching, techniques of discipline, and specialized remedial and counseling services. We rarely attend to the culture of the school, except in moments of crisis. Only after shootings in our schools, for example, have we acknowledged the problem of bullying, long a staple of peer culture in American junior high and high schools. Yet in spite of our awareness of the pain that bullying brings about, we have done little or nothing to address bullying at the cultural level. Instead, we have seen a rapid rise in metal detectors, lock-down procedures, zero-tolerance policies, and dress codes. We have speculated about the mysteries of the adolescent psyche. School officials have responded to the symptoms of violence but not to their underlying causes. Our superintendents, principals, teachers, and the wider public have difficulty seeing bullying and breaches of discipline such as cheating and vandalism as based in the school's culture. They perceive such problems in a gestalt that accentuates individual students but not the groups to which they belong. Until we change the culture of schools into democratic communities, these problems are likely to persist and our character education programs to flounder.

Kohlberg's Sociological Turn

Those not familiar with Kohlberg's contributions to moral education may be puzzled by his investment in an approach that places such a strong emphasis on the organization and culture of the school. Kohlberg became famous for his six-stage theory of moral judgment, a theory that grew out of Jean Piaget's cognitive developmental research. Kohlberg's stage theory provides a powerful tool for understanding how children and adolescents think about and resolve moral problems, and his theory has obvious educational implications. For example, if children reason differently from their teachers, then teachers have to tailor their moral instruction to the children's level. Moreover, if Kohlberg and Piaget are correct that children construct their moral reasoning through social interaction, then methods of moral education should treat children as active, not passive, learners. The most direct application of Kohlberg's moral psychology is the dilemma-discussion approach in which leaders encourage students through Socratic questioning to resolve moral dilemmas. Research shows that when used appropriately over an extended period, the dilemma-discussion approach is an effective and reliable way of promoting moral stage development.

When Kohlberg began his research on the moral stages as a doctoral student in the late 1950s, the majority of social scientists equated morality with the norms and values of a particular society. In this view, moral education is reduced to the socialization or internalization of a society's standards. Kohlberg, on the other hand, thought that morality is based on universal principles of justice. For him, moral education meant the cultivation of moral reasoning. Although Kohlberg believed that moral education deserved to be undertaken in school, he questioned the extent to which schools really helped children to develop their thinking. Kohlberg was fond of describing children as natural moral philosophers, but he was unsure whether teachers, accustomed to wielding unquestioned moral authority in the classroom, would be willing to engage in philosophical dialogue with their students. Kohlberg became involved personally in moral education only after one of his graduate students, Moshe Blatt, demonstrated that the dilemma-discussion approach produced measurable stage change.

Although Kohlberg came to education as a psychologist focused on individual moral development, his early writings about education reveal a nascent and growing interest in the organization and culture of the school, territory usually explored by sociologists. Reflecting on the implications of his dissertation research, Kohlberg suggests in his first article on education that effective moral education has to address the hierarchical structure of the classroom and school.[1] He finds that the moral reasoning of children from working-class backgrounds does not develop to the higher moral stages as frequently as that of their age peers. Noting that such development seemed to require taking the perspective of those in authority, Kohlberg recommends that schools provide opportunities for students to participate in decision-making.

Several years later in arguably his best essay on moral education, Kohlberg boldly concludes that in order to accomplish the goal of moral development schools must provide a special environment:

> The Platonic view that I have been espousing suggests something still revolutionary and frightening to me if not to you, that the schools would be radically different places if they took seriously the teaching of real knowledge of the good.[2]

Kohlberg describes the ideal school as a "little Republic" in which principles of justice and love are central. Kohlberg's "little Republic" would be ruled not by an aristocracy of philosopher-teachers, but by a democracy of teachers and students engaged in philosophical deliberation about the good of their community.

Kohlberg's theorizing took an even more decisive sociological turn

1. L. Kohlberg, "Moral Education in the School," *School Review* 74 (1966): 1–30.

2. L. Kohlberg, "Education for Justice: A Modern Restatement of the Platonic View," in N. Sizer and T. Sizer, eds., *Moral Education: Five Lectures* (Cambridge, Mass.: Harvard University Press, 1970): 83.

after a visit to an innovative Israeli Youth Aliyah Kibbutz high school program in 1969. In a little-known chapter with the revealing title "Cognitive Developmental Theory and the Practice of Collective Moral Education," Kohlberg advances a startling proposal: "Right now, Youth Aliyah Kibbutz youth group practice seems better than anything we conceive from our theory, and it is not revisions in practice, but revisions of the way of thinking about it that I am suggesting."[3] Earlier in his career, Kohlberg had joined Piaget in criticizing the collectivist moral education advocated by the great French sociologist, Emile Durkheim (1925–1973).[4] Kohlberg saw collectivist moral education as a form of authoritarian indoctrination that resulted in conformity. His observations of the functioning of a democratic kibbutz youth group, however, led him to distinguish Durkheim's collectivism from that practiced in the totalitarian Soviet Union. After his kibbutz visit, Kohlberg entertained the possibility that Durkheim's collectivist theory could be made compatible with democratic decision-making and that the student peer group could become a powerful resource for promoting development. Yet how this strange hybrid of cognitive developmental psychology and collectivist sociology might serve to guide practice remained a puzzle until Cluster School, the first experimental Just Community school, opened in 1974.

Kohlberg completed his sociological turn after working several years in the Cluster School. As I will illustrate, we learned, often the hard way, that changing the peer culture required much more than simply leading stimulating moral discussions. We had to seize every opportunity to convince students to see themselves as part of a cohesive community and to accept responsibility for each other and for Cluster's future. We had to help them to believe that Cluster's welfare depended

3. L. Kohlberg, "Cognitive Developmental Theory and the Practice of Collective Moral Education," in M. Wolins and M. Gottesman, eds., *Group Care: An Israeli Approach* (New York: Gordon and Breach, 1971): 370.

4. E. Durkheim, *Moral Education: A Study in the Theory and Application of the Sociology of Education* (New York: Free Press, 1925/1973).

on their willingness to uphold Cluster's disciplinary policies and to sacrifice themselves.

The Practice of Democracy

Democracy provides the means of communicating the vision of community and transforming that vision into a reality. Democracy also serves as the link between individual and collective development. The most important of the Just Community's democratic institutions was the weekly community meeting in which students and faculty met to discuss community problems and to adopt rules and policies. Decisions in the community meetings were made through direct participatory democracy, with each student and faculty member having an equal vote. Students and faculty prepared for the community meeting by meeting each week in advisory groups of a dozen or so students and one teacher. These meetings allowed everyone to discuss the issues that would come before the entire community; in effect they were dry runs for the larger community meeting. Infractions of rules and conflicts between students, or between students and teachers, were taken up in the discipline committee, which in later Just Community programs has been aptly renamed the fairness committee. This committee, whose membership rotated every few months, consisted mostly of students. Appeals of this committee's decisions went directly to the community meeting.

As we discovered in Cluster and rediscover each time we start a new Just Community program, establishing the institutions of participatory democracy is easy; achieving the ideal of democratic community is not. Living in a representative democracy, we have little experience deliberating in common about the rules and policies that affect our daily lives, and often less experience deliberating about the common good. We live in a time of widespread cynicism about democratic politics, cynicism that reaches down into our schools. We found in Cluster, and continue to find, that it takes almost an entire year for faculty and students to trust that the democratic process can work fairly for everyone. That kind of trust comes about only through actual experience. Faculty fears of a tyranny of the student majority and student fears of a sham democracy have, as we shall see, some basis, but they can be addressed.

The early days of Cluster were, by all accounts, at times chaotic. Teachers insisted that the first community meeting be dedicated to planning an innovative afternoon curriculum. They presented students with an impressive array of elective courses only to find that the students were less interested in designing the curriculum than they were testing the extent of their democratic power. One student interrupted the teacher-dominated discussion with a motion to make afternoon classes optional. A second quickly followed, and students asked for an immediate vote. Not surprisingly, the motion carried easily. As the students got up to leave, Kohlberg, noting that their vote was only a straw vote, stopped them.

At about the same time, Kohlberg arranged a field trip for the students to see a movie at Harvard, which was down the street from the high school. At a community meeting to prepare for the trip, Kohlberg explained that smoking would not be permitted in the auditorium where the movie would be shown and he made the trip conditional upon a democratic decision to prohibit smoking. The students readily agreed but when the movie began, students casually lit up their cigarettes. After waiting in vain for the teachers to intervene, Kohlberg stopped the projector and flicked on the lights. He expressed shock and wonder that students would so casually violate their democratically made rule. Kohlberg was less surprised that the students would break the rule than that the faculty failed to intervene. He quickly realized that this experiment in moral education would have to begin with the teachers, who were no more experienced with democratic community than were the students. Teachers tend to think of discipline dichotomously, as being either authoritarian or permissive, and to think of being democratic as being permissive. During the free-school movement of the 1970s, many teachers idealistically and naively believed that once the oppressive constraints of authoritarian discipline were withdrawn, students would naturally be cooperative and responsible. Teachers were generally reluctant to endorse rules of any type and preferred to establish guidelines and to deal with compliance issues on an informal, individual basis.

We viewed democracy very differently from most of those involved with the alternative school movement at that time. First of all, we insisted that attendance at community meetings be a nonnegotiable requirement for all students and faculty. Making democracy mandatory seemed contradictory, particularly to teachers and students in free schools. On the other hand, we believed that direct participatory democracy was the fundamental principle upon which the school is established. We also thought of democracy as a form of pedagogy. As did John Dewey (1916/1966), we regarded democratic participation as a means as well as an end of education.[5] We recognized that most high school students are not fully competent to shoulder the responsibilities of democratic participation. On the other hand, we believed that they could best acquire democratic competencies as well as a sense of civic engagement through democratic experience. We therefore adopted an apprenticeship model of democratic education advanced long ago by Horace Mann, the founder of the American public school. Mann called attention to the irony of having authoritarian schools in a democratic nation:

> In order that men may be prepared for self-government, their apprenticeship must begin in childhood . . . He who has been a serf until the day before he is twenty- one years of age, cannot be an independent citizen the day after; and it makes no difference whether he has been a serf in Austria or America. As the fitting apprenticeship for despotism consists in being trained for despotism, so the fitting apprenticeship for self-government consists in being trained to self-government.[6]

5. J. Dewey, *Democracy and Education* (New York: Free Press, 1916/1966).

6. H. Mann, *The Republic and the School: The Education of Free Men* (New York: Teachers College, Columbia University, 1845/1957): 58.

The apprenticeship model has two essential features. First, it is a learn-by-doing approach that gives students regular opportunities to practice democratic decision-making. Second, it is a training approach that provides direction and guidance. Although democracy involves an egalitarian relationship between teachers and students, an apprenticeship is by nature hierarchical. An apprenticeship in democracy may thus appear to be contradictory. Yet the hierarchy of an apprenticeship is primarily established, not through positional authority but through expertise and experience. In a democratic apprenticeship, the teachers' expertise is exercised primarily through their persuasiveness and organizational responsibility in establishing and maintaining democratic institutions.

We may ask, however, whether teachers can be both leaders and equal members of a democratic school. In his classic *The Moral Education of the Child*, Piaget (1932/1965) raises serious problems for such a view.[7] He postulates that there are two moralities of the child: a morality of constraint of the adult over the child and a morality of cooperation among children. A morality of constraint follows almost inevitably from the hierarchical relationship of adult to child. A morality of cooperation develops out of peer relationships. These moralities operate in diametrically different ways. A morality of constraint is one of subservient compliance to a superior authority—reason has no place in this morality because the child bases respect for authority on the mere fact of the adult's superior power. A morality of cooperation, on the other hand, is one of collaboration among equals—reason is central to this morality because the children must freely establish their own rules and norms. Piaget denounces the monarchical authority that leads teachers to foster mindless conformity in their students. Such an approach, he writes, ignores the facts of child development and fosters rebellion at worst and passivity at the very least.

7. J. Piaget, *The Moral Judgment of the Child* (New York: Free Press, 1965; original work published in 1932).

We agree with Piaget that adults can and often do get in the way of the development of children's moral judgment. As I noted earlier, Kohlberg's research on moral discussions showed that to be effective, teachers had to use a Socratic questioning approach. Nothing can short-circuit a discussion more quickly than a teacher who answers his or her own question or requires students to guess at the right answer. We believe that teachers have to engage students in serious moral dialogue, which entails careful listening as well as questioning. This means that teachers must set aside their roles as the authority who possesses the truth to assume the role of fellow inquirer. In a democratic school, this means that teachers should act as equal members of the group or, in Piaget's terms, as elder collaborators. When necessary, teachers should also act as facilitators of moral discussion and the democratic process. The apprenticeship model suggests that the teachers' role extends beyond that of facilitator to that of exemplar or leader.

The Teacher's Role

Only after several years of consultation at Cluster did we manage to articulate the complex role that teachers should play in the Just Community democracy. The role entailed maintaining a delicate balance between offering direction and releasing control. Teachers had to encourage students to feel a sense of ownership of the school while challenging them to strive for the ideals of community. At times, teachers had to withhold their own opinions in order to facilitate student discussion; at other times, the teachers had to speak out on behalf of the community, or sometimes on behalf of their own interests.

Kohlberg's thinking about the teacher's role was heavily influenced by his observations of the *madrich*, the adult leader in a kibbutz school. Kohlberg reported that through the *madrich's* skillful but subtle direction, the students formed an unusually cohesive and well-disciplined community. Kohlberg noted, "Underneath the informality of the *madrich* there is a considerable amount of iron, and this iron is based on the theory of collective education."[8] The *madrich* seldom gave orders or speeches, but he understood and made use of the power of the peer group. There is no clear counterpart to the *madrich* in the American education system. The *madrich* assumed some of the familiar functions of principal, counselor, and homeroom teacher, yet the *madrich's* major contribution was to work through the democratic process to involve students in building community.

Although we tried to help the Cluster teachers to adopt a role similar to that of the *madrich*, we had little initial success. Junior-high and high-school teachers see themselves primarily as responsible for teaching their subject, for example, history, science, or math. Unless they teach a civics education course, they do not see themselves as responsible for preparing students for democratic citizenship. Moreover, they are generally uncomfortable about their roles as disciplinarians. Most teachers think of discipline as control or management, a necessary but unpleasant way of securing the conditions that allow them to teach. Interviews that my students and I have conducted reveal that they have difficulty even imagining discipline as "the morality of the classroom" (Durkheim, 1925/1973) or discipline as an educational activity.[9] Before we were able to help the Cluster teachers forge their role in the Just Community approach, we had to persuade them that deliberating about disciplinary problems in a democratic context was worth the time and effort. We had to help them become aware of the value of listening to students rather than simply preaching to them.

I demonstrate the benefits as well as the challenge of envisioning a new disciplinary role for teachers with a simple example taken from a conventional junior high school. The teacher, Ms. Jones, was known as one of the best teachers in the junior high school. She related well to students and was interested in learning more about moral education.

8. See Kohlberg (1971): 358.

9. E. Durkheim, *Moral Education: A Study in the Theory and Application of the Sociology of Education* (New York: Free Press, 1925/1973): 1448.

In the middle of the school year, she discovered that one of her advanced students, Susan, had given her assignment to Joey, who had copied it. She swiftly punished Susan and Joey for cheating by giving them failing grades for the assignment, calling their parents, and excluding them from the monthly good-behavior pizza party. When I became aware of this incident, I thought that it might provide a teachable moment for Ms. Jones to explore the issue of copying assignments with her class and maybe even for her to involve students in making a rule prohibiting such collaboration as well as more serious kinds of cheating. I suggested to Ms. Jones that the students who cheated may not have felt that what they had done was really wrong, and recommended that she hold a class discussion about such copying to ascertain what her students thought. If her students did not think that it was wrong, then she might have to reconsider her punitive response and, at the very least, lead a moral discussion on cheating.

Ms. Jones agreed to the discussion although she expressed skepticism about its necessity. The following day she asked the class, "Who here believes that lending your class assignment to another student isn't cheating?" The students snickered but not a hand went up. Ms. Jones concluded by reminding her students that the rules she had distributed in writing at the beginning of the school year clearly forbade such cheating, and she expected no more incidents. After class dismissal, another student was overheard asking Susan to let her copy her homework over the lunch period.

This example illustrates the futility of an authoritarian approach to discipline. Ms. Jones established and enforced the classroom rules without involving the students. However, she did not believe that she was simply asserting her authority as a teacher or that she was demanding obedience to an arbitrary or irrational rule. The purpose of homework, mastery of the material, is undermined by copying someone else's answers. Copying, moreover, is dishonest. Students surely know or at least can readily recognize the point that this is true. Would explaining the educational benefits of doing one's own work or the importance of honesty have made any difference in Susan's or anyone else's behavior? In my view, the problem was not a matter of student ignorance or ill will but a problem of the peer culture. Students did not think about copying in moral terms. In fact, the students had developed a norm among themselves in which copying was understood as helping. In order to change the peer culture, Ms. Jones would first have had to invite her students to share their views on the matter. What would students have replied if Ms. Jones had asked them what they thought about copying? When I later asked Susan why she cheated, she objected, "Cheating? I thought that I was helping, that I was being a Mother Teresa." If Susan had participated in a genuine moral discussion with her peers, she would likely have defended her action as being harmless at worst (Joey usually did his own work) and altruistic at best (not only was she helping a friend who had fallen behind but also all the students in the advanced group who had to wait for him to finish). Ms. Jones would have been in a good position to suggest to Susan and her peers that a better way of helping Joey may have been to encourage him to finish the work on his own. Ms. Jones could also have discussed the matters of honesty and the importance of trust in the classroom. Eventually Ms. Jones could have asked the class to come up with a rule for assignments to express the values of working on one's own, honesty, and trust.

In sketching out how Ms. Jones could have acted, I wish not to blame her. She is to be commended for the moral seriousness with which she responded to the incident in her class. Many teachers might have looked the other way or failed to realize that moral issues were at stake. Ms. Jones's response was, nevertheless, ineffectual—possibly even counterproductive. She could have acted differently with a far greater probability of success, but unfortunately could not perceive another way of acting. Teachers are neither prepared for nor expected to lead moral discussions about classroom discipline, let alone to organize their classrooms to provide an apprenticeship in democracy. Teachers are not trained to play the role of the *madrich* in mobilizing students to build a better community to attend to the peer culture. Ms. Jones punished Susan and Joey, assuming that this would deter them and others in the future. The punishment, however, appeared to deter no one except Susan, who refused to lend her homework the next time she was asked. When I later asked her why she did not lend her homework, she stated simply that she did not want to get in trouble. She confided that she felt angry and betrayed, and that her friends supported her. It appears that the deterrent approach not only failed to influence Susan's moral reasoning but also alienated Susan and her peers from the teacher, and to some extent from the school itself.

Analyzing the effectiveness of the conventional classroom management approach to discipline from the standpoint of moral education will, I believe, lead to the exploration of alternatives such as the Just Community approach, which address student culture as well as moral reasoning. We need to be able to bridge the culture gap, identified long ago by Willard Waller, who depicted teachers and their students as living two different, almost impenetrable social worlds.[10] The students, he found, tend to bond together in strong primary groups, which teachers try to control from the outside, as it were, through extrinsic rewards and punishments. As I have illustrated, the mechanisms of extrinsic control only further alienate the student culture. In order to break down the barriers between teachers and students, teachers need to appeal to the student culture from the inside. This is what the Just Community approach tries to do by asking teachers to share power as well as responsibility in enabling students to build a cohesive moral community.

The teacher's role in the Just Community encompasses more than that of facilitator and elder collaborator—teachers must be willing to guide and to lead. As was evident from the earliest Cluster community meetings, teachers need to impress upon students the need for careful deliberation before coming to a decision. Teachers may also be called upon to give direction to discussions by speaking out on behalf of the

10. W. Waller, *The Sociology of Teaching* (New York: John Wiley & Sons, 1932).

ideals of the community. Kohlberg played this role in the early days of Cluster, and we wanted faculty to assume it as soon as possible; we conceived this role as that of advocate. In formalizing it, we were all too aware that teachers could easily abuse it. On the other hand, we recognized that the Cluster democracy would flounder without Kohlberg and the teachers consistently appealing to the two pillars of the Just Community approach: democracy and community. These pillars are not just descriptive aspects of an institutional reality, they are normative ideals. Cluster had to become a democracy by developing depth of participation, and a community by developing bonds of caring, trust, and responsibility.

Building Community through Collective Norms

I conclude this chapter by discussing our understanding of community and how we tried to build it through establishing what we called collective norms. We defined community as a group in which members value their common life for its own sake, distinguishing community from an association in which relationships among the members are valued instrumentally. The kind of community that we endeavored to develop through the Just Community approach was one characterized by shared expectations for a high degree of solidarity, care, trust, and participation in group activities. These expectations did not arise spontaneously but had to be carefully cultivated over time.

We discovered early that the opportunity to vote on rules was insufficient to change student behavior. Students were accustomed to having rules against disrupting class, fighting, stealing, and skipping class; but these rules were enforced by the teachers through personal charisma or threat. We wanted to get the student peer group behind the rule. This meant that students would have to view the rules as expressing the shared expectations of the community. How could one lead students to have enough of a sense of ownership of the school so that they cared about the welfare of the community as a whole? Making rules democratically after considerable discussion helped enormously. Over time, students felt a sense of ownership of the school and increasingly accepted responsibility for resolving disciplinary problems, yet the students typically tried to address problems extrinsically through the threat of punishment rather than intrinsically through appealing to each other's commitment to the community's core values.

We first used the term "collective norm" to describe the shared expectations that we were trying to engender through community meeting discussions when we compared transcripts from two community meetings focused on the issue of stealing (see Power, Higgins, and Kohberg).[11] The first meeting took place during Cluster's first year and resulted in a rule prohibiting stealing; the second, the following year, resulted in a decision that everyone should chip in to reimburse a theft victim in the school. We believed that a sense of community had clearly developed from the first to the second year. We were hard-pressed, however, to describe the change in the community's culture to distinguish it from the stage change simultaneously occurring in the individual student's moral reasoning.

When stealing first occurred in Cluster, the students were nonchalant. "School isn't a place for trusting stuff, even at Cluster. Community or not, if you want something, you'll take it. It [stealing] goes to show you can't be too friendly." When Kohlberg attempted to arouse a feeling of moral indignation about the lack of trust and community, a student shot back, "Just because a few things were stolen, you don't have to cry about it." Many students seemed to think that stealing was wrong simply because it was a violation of one's concrete right of ownership (what Kohlberg scored as Stage 2 reasoning). Others voiced the more advanced insight that stealing was a violation of interpersonal trust (Stage 3): "I know lots of people who steal . . . and you really feel bad about that." Even those students conceded that there was not much that could

11. F. C. Power, A. Higgins, and L. Kohlberg, *Lawrence Kohlberg's Approach to Moral Education* (New York: Columbia University Press, 1989).

be done about stealing besides establishing a punishment that might deter potential thieves. By the following year, the focus of the discussion had shifted radically. Many more students spoke up than in the previous year, and the majority seemed to be invested in Kohlberg's vision of community.

> *Phyllis:* It is everyone's fault that she don't have no money. It was stolen because people don't care about the community. [They think] they are all individuals and don't have to be included in the community. Everybody should care that she got her money stolen [and therefore] we [those students in Phyllis's advisory group] decided to give her money back to her.
>
> *Bob:* That somebody stole the money is pretty bad, but to me, that I have to pay because she lost her money is like someone robbing a bank and the bank owner comes to my door and asks me to pay a couple of bucks because they lost their money. That's crazy!
>
> *Albert:* What's your definition of community?
>
> *Bob:* My definition of community is that people can help one another right there. But I didn't say nothing about giving money out.
>
> *Albert:* The money was lost or stolen or whatever and it's not really to return the money, it is to help someone in the community altogether. I think it would be the first really community thing that we have ever done, really. It doesn't concern the money, it concerns community action.
>
> *Peggy:* I think that if Bob feels so strongly about [giving] his fifteen cents to Monica that he shouldn't belong in this community. I am sure that if it was his money he would feel the other way around. He wouldn't want nine dollars taken from him, he would be crying.[12]

Kohlberg and I were especially intrigued with Phyllis's comments because, in addition to expressing her own point of view, she seemed to be speaking on behalf of the Cluster community. According to Kohlberg's stage theory, Phyllis saw the problem of stealing as more than a concrete loss of property (Stage 2), but as a lack of interpersonal caring

12. Ibid., 113–114.

(Stage 3). Albert and Peggy clearly agreed with Phyllis for similar, Stage-3 reasons. Kohlberg and I found that on the whole, there were far more instances of Stage-3 reasoning in this second meeting than in the first, suggesting that the modal stage of the group may have developed from Stage 2 to Stage 3. Yet this depiction of the change between the two years failed to capture the way in which Phyllis, Albert, and Peggy appeared to be speaking as representatives of the Cluster community and not just for themselves as individuals. Phyllis says, "Everybody should care that she got her money stolen" and earlier that the theft was "everyone's fault." Phyllis is clearly voicing more than her personal opinion about stealing. She is expressing a norm that she believes binds her fellow students not only as individuals but as members of the community.

Phyllis, moreover, is not merely proposing that the community adopt norms of trust and caring as Kohlberg did in the previous year. Phyllis assumes that the community has accepted these norms and expresses disappointment that some members have not lived up to them. Her statements as well as Albert's and Peggy's suggest that the culture of Cluster had changed dramatically. Over the course of a year, Cluster appeared to have developed from a collection of individuals with very low aspirations for their common life to a community in which members are expected to care for and trust one another.

How can we be certain that Phyllis and others represented the wider group? There were students like Bob in Cluster, who did not understand or did not agree with the concept of community that Phyllis, Albert, and Peggy advanced. The best that we could hope for was that increasing numbers of students would share a vision of Cluster and ask each other to begin to realize that vision. Each time a class graduated and a new class joined the school, that vision would have to be communicated and the group's norms renegotiated. Looking over that second meeting, we were encouraged that most of the students who spoke sided with Phyllis, Albert, and Peggy, and that the vast majority of the community voted in favor of Phyllis's motion for restitution. Interviews with students that year confirmed that, indeed, Phyllis had spoken for the majority of the students. A consensus was emerging about what membership in the Cluster community entailed.

Through the process of identifying the development of collective norms, we came to understand more clearly what the Just Community approach demands and why it is so counter-cultural. If we really want schools to become communities characterized by trust, caring, and shared responsibility, teachers and students must engage in serious moral dialogue about their common life. They have to use the democratic process as a means of communicating a vision and establishing shared expectations. In making and enforcing rules, they need to ask themselves whether their decisions reflect a commitment to foster the welfare and solidarity of the community or whether their decisions reflect their own interests or that of a subgroup.

Conclusion

As I illustrated in the example of Susan's cheating, teachers do not habitually deliberate about disciplinary and school life issues with students, nor build community, by asking students to make sacrifices for worthy ideals. Ironically, Bob's depiction of the school as a bank may well be accurate for conventional schools. We join banks for instrumental, self-serving purposes; banks cannot ask us to be responsible for each other's or the bank's welfare. The more schools resemble banks, the less effective they are in fostering moral development. Our experience with the Just Community approach in Cluster and in subsequent projects suggests that schools can buck the culture; they do not have to be like banks.

Some have asked whether the Just Community programs have more than a temporary, context-specific influence on their students. Why focus on developing collective norms within a particular school? What happens when students leave the community? I maintain that the experience of democratically participating in moral community fosters general confidence in the democratic process and commitment to the common good. There is now some quantitative evidence to support me. Grady found that ten years after their graduation, Cluster alumnae and alumni were more likely than their peers to have an interest in politics and national affairs; to have voted in local elections; to have a concern for local government decisions; and to have worked with others in a community to solve community problems.[13]

There is now an unprecedented commitment at the federal, state, and local levels to promote character education in our nation's schools. As programs proliferate, we should be wary of programs that proclaim the virtues in abstract and superficial ways but do not touch students' hearts or minds. We should be sensitive to the fact that the values that we espouse in such programs are often not the values that are reflected in the institutional and cultural life of the school. We should be concerned that although we live in a democratic society, our schools are not democratic. If the Just Community approach seems radical today, it is because our schools are not the places that they should be and we have not prepared our teachers and our principals as we should. The Just Community approach is radical in the sense that it is rooted in the principles of democracy and community upon which our nation stands. We should, like Kohlberg, ask our schools to become "little republics," challenging our students to commit themselves to a higher good and in so doing fostering the development of moral responsibility and civic engagement.

13. E. A. Grady, "After Cluster School: A Study of the Impact in Adulthood of a Moral Education Intervention Project." Unpublished doctoral dissertation, Harvard University, 1994.

Whose Values Anyway?

Anne Colby

TWO POWERFUL CURRENTS flowing through contemporary American higher education are pulling the field in different directions. The stronger of the two is a trend toward specialization and commercialization. This current is leading to the creation of an education industry that is responsive to market pressures, concentrating on preparing workers suited to American industry and giving students skills to compete economically so they can lead more comfortable, affluent lives. In this model, students are treated as consumers who invest time and money in higher education in order to receive future economic benefits. This increasingly powerful corporate model of higher education imports the values assumptions, language, and administrative policies of the business world, including marketing and market research, corporate management strategies, and aggressive public-relations campaigns. This conception of higher education is part of a longer-term historical change in the way higher education's purposes are understood, a shift away from an earlier conception of the public purposes of higher education and toward a more individualistic, technical, and morally disinterested understanding of those purposes.

At the same time that universities move in this specialized and narrowly market-driven direction, we see a groundswell of interest in higher education's capacity to contribute to stronger communities, a more responsive democratic system, and more engaged citizens. Critics from outside and within the academy are joining a chorus of calls to revitalize the public purposes of higher education, including educating for students' moral and civic development, as well as technical and more narrowly intellectual learning. The urgency of these calls is reinforced by a society-wide concern about the extent to which citizens, especially young people, are disengaged from public life.

I believe there is reason for serious concern about higher education's move toward a corporate and individualistic approach, and that we need to support the growing but still somewhat peripheral movement to make higher education a force for strengthening American democracy. Borrowing ideas and practices from the business world may increase the efficiency and effectiveness of institutions of higher education in some ways, and has no doubt made schools more responsive to the interests of their students. Heavy reliance on a corporate model, however, risks obscuring important differences between profit-making businesses and nonprofit educational institutions. Although financial viability is an obvious prerequisite to the continued existence of a college or university, if used as the overriding criterion for setting and evaluating priorities and policies, it will subordinate concern for many important learning outcomes and public purposes to a narrow understanding of educational goals.

Many kinds of social institution play important roles in educating citizens. Religious organizations and other voluntary associations, the media, and education at the elementary and secondary levels are among the most important of these. But higher education is critical because universities and colleges are the institutions most clearly charged with leading the development of new and deeper understanding through research and scholarship, and preparing new generations by teaching not only information and skills, but their significance for personally and collectively creating the future. Higher education has tremendous opportunities as a positive force in society as it reaches an ever-larger segment of the population, including virtually all leaders in government and the private sector. It is a powerful influence in shaping individuals' relationships with each other and their communities, and we need to ensure that its influence is constructive rather than corrosive. There is no question that higher education has begun to respond to these concerns. In response to calls for a renewal of civic engagement and social responsibility, colleges and universities are becoming more directly involved in efforts to address social problems in their local communities, for example by developing partnerships with local schools or establishing public forums for discussion of political and policy issues.

In addition to this kind of institutional engagement, some colleges and universities have begun to place greater emphasis on student outcomes that concern public service, civic participation and leadership, and humane or ethical values and behavior. This is apparent in the proliferation of curricular and extracurricular programs designed to foster the development of students' moral and civic responsibility, such as ethics across the curriculum, service-learning, and community service programs such as alternative spring break.

Educational leaders have established a number of national networks to support this kind of work, the most visible of which are networks concerned with service-learning, such as Campus Compact and the Learn and Serve Higher Education initiative of the Corporation for National Service. In addition to the development of these specialized networks, national organizations of higher education such as the Association of American Colleges and Universities and the American Association of Higher Education are placing these concerns at the center of their agendas. Communication about this work is broadening its reach as national conferences are held on college student values and education for civic participation.

But even as this movement to reinstate the public purposes of higher education strengthens, there are powerful points of resistance to it. Whether the movement can significantly temper the trend toward education as a commodity for individual advancement is very much in question. Higher education could continue to drift loose from its moorings as an institution for the public good and move farther down the path toward market-driven training unconcerned with the education of the student as person and citizen. A number of arguments are raised over and over to justify giving up higher education's moral and civic purposes, to make these goals seem obsolete in the contemporary world. These arguments are widespread and threaten to nip in the bud the revival of the public purposes of higher education, or at least to keep it very much on the margin of academic life. This essay will argue that these objections are misplaced, ill-informed, and incorrect.

Argument: Higher Education Has No Business Addressing Values

The first of these arguments is that higher education has no business addressing issues of values: it should be value-neutral, impart knowledge and skills, and leave questions of moral and civic values to the family, the church, and political institutions. Although this recommendation may seem plausible at first glance, closer scrutiny makes it clear that educational institutions cannot be value-neutral. For decades educators have recognized the power of the hidden curriculum in schools and the moral messages it carries.[1] The hidden curriculum is the (largely unexamined) practices through which the school and its teachers operate—maintain discipline, assign grades and other rewards, and man-

1. Lawrence Kohlberg, "Indoctrination and Relativity in Value Education," *Xygon* 6 (1971): 285–309; P. W. Jackson, *Life in the Classroom* (New York: Holt, Rinehart and Winston, 1968); G. D. Fenstermacher, "Some Moral Considerations on Teaching as a Profession," in J. Goodlad, R. Soder, and K. Sirotnik, eds., *The Moral Dimensions of Teaching* (San Francisco: Jossey-Bass, 1990): 130–54.

age their relationships with their students and each other. Although most research on the hidden curriculum has been directed toward elementary and secondary education, the concept applies equally to higher education. If college students see faculty rewarded for pursuing their own professional prestige rather than caring for others or the institution, if they are subjected to competitive climates in which one student's success contributes to another's failure, if they are confronted with institutional hypocrisy, they themselves can become cynical and self-interested. On the other hand, when faculty are scrupulously honest, fair, and caring with their students and approach their scholarship with integrity, they teach powerful moral lessons of a very different sort.

In addition to these values messages in relations between faculty and students, messages of instrumental individualism and materialism are more and more prevalent in the broader institutional and peer cultures on many campuses. The commercialization of higher education, including corporate sponsorship of faculty and student research, corporate underwriting of certain courses, advertising on websites, and exclusive beverage-pouring rights given to products such as Coke or Pepsi at sports and other events, though it provides some institutional benefits, also acts to reinforce themes of materialism and commercialism that are pervasive in the general culture. Few would deny the influence of commercial interests on the informal learning contexts in which college students are immersed through television, film, music, and other media. When higher education reinforces these cultural trends, it may appear to be value-neutral, but clearly it is not.

Academic disciplines also embody values assumptions that contribute to shaping students' frames of reference, though these assumptions are often unexamined and thus invisible. The preponderance of research in economics and much of that in political science, for example, build on a model that assumes rational choice, which is seldom subjected to critical analysis in the teaching of these disciplines. This model of human behavior assumes that individuals always seek to maximize their perceived interests and that social phenomena represent the aggregate of individuals employing this self-interested strategy. A similar perspective is fostered by research and theory in other fields such as sociobiology and some approaches within psychology, which also assume a self-interested or mechanistic view of human nature. An unquestioned reliance on these models of human behavior can result in a normalization of self-interestedness, contributing to the common belief that individuals are always fundamentally motivated by self-interest, that altruism or genuine concern for others' welfare are illusory, and that failing to act strategically to achieve one's own self-interested goals would be foolish.[2]

In many disciplines, including such wide-ranging fields as literature, genetics, engineering, and business, moral issues are integral to the material, and teaching that does not address them is itself a lesson in a particular way to orient to complex, multidimensional material. James Rest, Muriel Bebeau, Janet Walker, and others have written about the central role of interpretation and sensitivity to moral issues in moral understanding and behavior.[3] In a recent paper Janet Walker explores the implications of the fact that most life situations are inherently ambiguous, their moral significance underdetermined by available facts. In order to find meaning and clarity amid this ambiguity, people develop habits of moral interpretation and intuition through which they perceive the world. In effect, people with different habits of moral interpretation live in worlds that can be very different, although they have much in common, and these worlds present different opportunities and imperatives for moral action.

2. For a discussion of these issues in the field of economics, see Myra H. Strober, "Rethinking Economics through a Feminist Lens," *American Economic Review* (May 1994): 143–47.

3. See, for example: J. Rest, *Development in Judging Moral Issues* (Minneapolis: University of Minnesota Press, 1979); M. J. Bebeau, "Influencing the Moral Dimension of Dental Practice," in J. Rest and D. Narvaez, eds., *Moral Development in the Professions* (Hillsdale, N.J.: Lawrence Erlbaum Press, 1994); J. Walker, "Choosing Biases, Using Power and Practicing Resistance: Moral Development in a World without Certainty," *Human Development* 43:3(2000): 135–94.

Over and over in their undergraduate careers, students encounter course material that raises salient moral issues, but in most classrooms these issues are consistently set aside as irrelevant to understanding the material. This constitutes systematic, though unintentional, training in habits of moral interpretation that teach students to turn a blind eye toward the moral issues implicit in many situations. In these and many other ways, educational institutions convey values and moral messages to their students. This is unavoidable. Given this reality, it seems preferable for these institutions to examine their values and make more conscious, deliberate choices about what they convey to students. This brings us back into controversy, since in making these choices, educational institutions are forced to confront the pluralistic nature of our society and thus of our faculty and student bodies.

Argument: Whose Values?

One effort to remain apparently value-neutral while educating responsible citizens is through the cultivation of "value-free" or "content-free" skills of intellectual discipline, critical thinking, and analytical reasoning. These goals are, after all, at the heart of higher education's academic identity. Although fostering civic participation or engagement is also quite likely to be regarded as safely value-neutral and thus theoretically relatively benign, in practice it raises questions about the political ideologies that lie behind it, and therefore begins to encounter resistance. The most heated objections arise relative to approaches that include concern for morality, character, and values along with attention to civic engagement and responsibility. Questions of whose values, assumptions of indoctrination, and complaints that "this is not the proper role of higher education," begin in earnest as soon as the word "morality" is used.

Why not, then, focus on the development of skills needed for effective citizenship, including such undeniably valuable capacities as critical thinking, and leave the development of values and morality to the private sphere? My colleagues and I have argued elsewhere that this is neither desirable nor even possible. To assume that cultivation of core academic capacities such as analytical thinking and disinterested scientific and scholarly expertise is sufficient to produce responsible citizens who will devote themselves to the common good of society begs the question of motivation to do so and flies in the face of extensive evidence of contemporary civic and political disengagement, particularly among young people. There is plenty of evidence that recipients of this kind of education are choosing more and more to apply their analytic skills and professional expertise to their own personal advancement, and the educational approach described here does not presume to address that trend.

Can we focus on education for civic responsibility and thereby avoid addressing the most controversial area of *moral* values? This move will not work either, because education for democratic participation necessarily engages moral issues. Our democratic principles, including tolerance and respect for others, procedural impartiality, and concern for both the rights of the individual and the welfare of the group, are all grounded in moral principles.

Likewise, the problems that the civically engaged citizen must confront always include strong moral themes—for example, fair access to resources such as housing, the moral obligation to consider future generations in making environmental policy, and the conflicting claims of multiple stakeholders in community decision-making. None of these issues can be resolved adequately without a consideration of moral questions. A person can become civically and politically active without good judgment and a strong moral compass, but it is hardly wise to promote that kind of involvement. Because civic responsibility is inescapably threaded with moral values, higher education must aspire to foster both moral and civic maturity and must confront educationally the many links between them.

This brings us to the second common objection to undergraduate moral and civic education: we live in a pluralistic society, so there is no legitimate way to determine which (or whose) values ought to be conveyed. This objection takes two forms. The first derives from the diversity that characterizes contemporary American society, which comprises people of many cultural backgrounds and traditions, religions, and political perspectives. The second reflects the recognition that within any given cultural tradition, there are reasonable variations and disagreements about many moral, civic, political, and religious issues.

In addressing these concerns, it is important to distinguish between pluralism and moral relativism. A pluralistic view of morality assumes that two or more incommensurable moral frameworks can be justified. This does not mean that *any* possible moral framework is justifiable, only that there are multiple valid moral frameworks that cannot be reduced to a single system. In contrast, moral relativism holds that there is no basis at all for distinguishing among moral positions, that none can be considered any more or less valid than any other. Few critics of moral and civic education are relativistic in this sense. If they were, they would not be able to argue with any credibility that universities ought not indoctrinate their students with an arbitrary set of values, since this argument is itself a moral claim that, presumably, they feel they can justify on moral grounds.

For many years, anthropologists have documented the plural norms that exist in different cultures throughout the world (diversity in what people do or believe they ought to do). Some have argued that this diversity of norms is superficial and, once its meaning is understood, it reduces to underlying moral principles common to all cultures. Others have tried to show that cultural diversity reflects fundamental differences in moral perspectives, so that the values most important in one culture are much less central or salient in another. Richard Shweder has done extensive field work to document the fact that moral concepts such as autonomy, individual rights, and justice, which are central to American and European conceptions of morality, are, in other cultures such as India, overshadowed by other more elaborated and salient moral concepts such as duty, sacrifice, and loyalty.[4] It is important to note, however, that even in anthropological research documenting cultural differences in moral values, there are boundaries to the range of what is seen to count as an ultimate moral good, and that even very different moral perspectives include (though they do not stress) the values of the other perspectives. Differences in moral frames of reference are best seen as differences in how a common set of base values are ordered when they conflict, and which of those values are more salient in practice. Even anthropologists who believe there is fundamental moral heterogeneity across cultures do not generally believe in extreme and unqualified cultural relativism. Even very different (and fundamentally incommensurate) moral perspectives build on a base set of moral goods or virtues that human beings have in common. Presumably, these commonalities will be even stronger within a single country, even a culturally heterogeneous and pluralistic country such as the United States.

How do we identify the moral commonalities or shared values that constitute a foundation on which American institutions of higher education can build consensus, while recognizing that the shared moral values often come into conflict with each other and that individuals and subcultures create different hierarchies among them? One important source of a common core of values for American higher education derives from the responsibility to educate for citizenship that most institutions acknowledge, even when it does not shape their practices to any significant degree. This responsibility is clear in public institutions. But even private colleges and universities receive public support, if only by virtue of their tax-exempt status, and almost all college and university mission statements refer to their responsibility to educate for leadership and contribution to society. The responsibility to prepare citizens for participation in a democratic system implies that some

4. R. Shweder, "True Ethnography: The Lore, the Law, and the Lure," in R. Jessor, A. Colby, and R. Shweder, eds., *Ethnography and Human Development* (Chicago: University of Chicago Press, 1996): 15–52.

values, including some *moral* values, ought to be represented in these institutions' educational goals. These values include mutual respect and tolerance, concern for the rights and welfare of individuals and the community, recognition that each individual is part of the larger social fabric, and a commitment to civil and rational discourse and procedural impartiality.

Universities' educational and scholarly missions also entail a set of core values. Few would dispute that higher education ought to embody the values of intellectual integrity and concern for truth. The academic enterprise would be fatally compromised if these values ceased to guide scholarship, teaching, and learning, however imperfect the guidance may be in practice. Equally central to an institution of scholarship and higher education are the ideals of open-mindedness, willingness to listen to and take seriously the ideas of others, and ongoing public discussion of contested issues.

Beyond this generic set of core values derived from the civic and intellectual purposes of higher education, some private colleges (and even a few public) stand for more specific moral, cultural, or religious values. The particular missions of these institutions and their implications for their educational programs must be made clear to prospective students and faculty. The most obvious examples are religiously affiliated colleges and universities that offer faith-based education in many denominations. Among public institutions, military academies are mandated to educate military officers, so their values are defined in reference to this goal. Other public colleges were established to serve particular populations, such as (American Indian) tribal colleges, which often explicitly acknowledge special values such as traditional tribal values in their curricula and programs.

If the values on which there is broad consensus within an institution are taken seriously, they constitute strong guiding principles for programs of moral and civic development in higher education. Even so, they leave open to debate the application of these principles to many particular situations. Especially in institutions that stand for a commitment to rational public discourse, as higher education must, discussion of the most difficult questions of conflicting values can and should be left open to debate. Moral and civic education provides the tools for such debate. This means that we need not begin with agreement on the most difficult and controversial cases of conflict between values. This makes it possible to reach a consensus on the initial set of core values.

Some critics may agree that, in principle, this approach to undergraduate education would be a good thing, but fear that in practice moral and civic education programs carry unacknowledged political and ideological baggage. These fears come from all points on the political spectrum, with terms like morality and character raising concerns about conservative influences and references to social justice or social change eliciting fears of liberal political agendas. It is important to be vigilant against educational practices that suppress a diversity of perspectives, and when abuses occur, it is both ethically and educationally indefensible. In my experience, however, most people engaged in college-level moral and civic education are aware of these risks and careful to guard against abuses.

In a project of the Carnegie Foundation for the Advancement of Teaching, several colleagues and I visited colleges and universities of all sorts that have made moral and civic education a priority, and have reviewed the work of many more. In our visits to even the most specialized institutions, we were surprised by the consistency with which faculty took care to ensure that multiple points of view were heard, and encouraged students to question and think through the assumptions in the dominant institutional culture. At Messiah College, a strongly Christian college of the Brethren in Christ Church, students often enter college not having questioned their faith and with little experience of people from other denominations. The faculty, who are charged with helping students explore the relationship between reason and faith, try to shake students up, encourage them to think for themselves, and push them out of their comfort zone. At the United States Air Force Academy, students understand that their future roles as military officers are subject to military command and military law, but they are also taught to disobey unlawful orders. This means that cadets have to develop the capacity for mature, independent judgment in complex and ambiguous situations, even within the military chain of command. At Portland State University, an urban institution in the politically liberal city of Portland, Oregon, faculty teaching service-learning courses meet regularly to talk about how to make sure all voices are heard in their discussions of moral, political, and policy issues.

Every institution we visited shares a central concern for student capacities inimical to any effort to impose a particular party line. These capacities include openness to reason, ability to communicate effectively, tolerance of perspectives different from one's own, clarity of thought and critical thinking, and capacity for moral discourse across points of view. With the exception of honor codes that require adherence to standards of honesty, the central pedagogies and other programs intended to foster moral and civic responsibility in these institutions are self-consciously noncoercive. In part because they are encouraged to think independently, the students we observed did not appear reluctant to resist if they thought a faculty member or another student was trying to impose his or her views. There may be abuses of these principles by individual faculty, or by institutions that we did not review, but this kind of abuse can occur whether the development of students' moral and civic responsibility are explicit goals of the institution or not. Urging institutions of higher education to be explicit and self-conscious in these efforts, to open their educational practices to public view, and to join a national conversation about these practices with a diverse range of other institutions is more likely to minimize the abuses of power the critics fear than is attempting to run a value-free institution. If pursued thoughtfully, an approach that brings these issues into public debate and discussion should allow us to reappropriate words such as morality, character, patriotism, and social justice across ideological lines and open communication about what they mean and what their implications are for difficult contemporary social issues.

The irony in the charge that moral and civic education imposes arbitrary values on students is that these values-based goals of liberal education are the best protection from indoctrination throughout life. Helping students develop the capacity for critical thinking, teaching them to be open-minded and interested in pursuing ideas, requiring them to back up their claims and to expect others to do the same, and encouraging them to be knowledgeable and accustomed to thinking about moral, civic, and political issues puts them in the strongest position to think independently about their positions and commitments. The more they think about these things and learn to argue them through, the less susceptible they are to indoctrination.

Argument: College Is Too Late for Moral and Civic Education

Another common set of objections to moral and civic education at the college level is that college students are now more likely to be seen as adults than they were in the early to mid-twentieth century. As higher education has become accessible to a larger segment of the population, the profile of college students has changed. The dominant template of pre-World War II higher education was private institutions educating full-time students from affluent families in residential settings. This is now a small sector of American undergraduate education. Currently, more than three out of four undergraduates are commuter students.[5] A near-majority of undergraduates today do not come to college or university directly from high school. They are older than their predecessors, work part-time, and are part-time undergraduates. Many are married and are parents. These important realities need to be taken into account as we design college-level programs to foster moral and civic responsibility.

5. U.S. Bureau of the *Census, Statistical Abstract of the United States*: 1998, 118th ed. (Springfield, Va.: National Technical Information Services, 1998).

This growing age diversity joins another trend toward recognizing college students' adult status. Until the early 1970s, many residential colleges and universities operated in loco parentis, that is, were charged with acting in a parental role toward their students by the imposition of parietal hours and rules over a wide range of other behavioral issues. A central purpose of this quasi-parental role was to ensure students' compliance with social and moral norms. As students in the 1960s and 1970s became more politicized, they demanded treatment as adults and much greater autonomy and self-regulation. Within less than a decade, there were few campuses on which the policies of in loco parentis were still in effect. This shift, along with the growing diversity in their ages and life situations, means that for many purposes, undergraduate students are now generally considered to be adults rather than adolescents.[6]

This has led critics to argue that by the time students are in college it is too late to affect their values and character, since moral character is assumed to be already fully established by then. There is clear research evidence that this assumption is incorrect. First, with reference to traditional undergraduates of ages eighteen to twenty-two or so, all of the major developmental theorists point to this period, which is often considered to represent the transition to adulthood, as a time of great moral and ideological exploration, ferment, and consolidation.[7] At this time

6. We recognize that, especially since the passage of the GI Bill after World War II, there have always been some older students in American colleges and universities. Even so, until the last several decades the dominant image of college students in the public mind has been that of young people not yet prepared to take responsibility for themselves. Some influential psychological theorists such as Erik Erikson and Marcia called this period a "moratorium" between adolescence and adulthood. See E. Erikson, *Identity, Youth and Crisis* (New York: Norton, 1968) and J. E. Marcia, "Identity in Adolescence," in J. Adelson, ed., *Handbook of Adolescent Psychology* (New York: Wiley, 1980).

7. E. Erikson, *Identity, Youth, and Crisis* (New York: Norton, 1968); William Perry, Jr. *Forms of Intellectual and Ethical Development in the College Years* (New York: Holt, Rinehart, and Winston, 1968); Lawrence Kohlberg, *The Psychology of Moral Development* (San Francisco: Harper & Row, 1984); J. Loevinger, *Ego Development* (San Francisco: Jossey-Bass, 1976).

in their lives, young people question their epistemological, moral, political, and religious assumptions, make critical career and other life choices, and rethink their sense of who they are and what is important to them. There could hardly be a time more ripe for moral growth.

For older students, the relevant psychological literature is the extensive work done in recent decades on adult and life span development. Although experiences in childhood and adolescence are clearly important in shaping individuals' moral judgment, identities, and behavior, it is clear that for many people moral development continues well into adulthood. The most sophisticated level of moral thinking in Kohlberg's developmental scheme, postconventional moral judgment, does not occur until early adulthood and continues to increase at least until the end of formal education, even beyond, for those people who continue to participate in activities that challenge their moral thinking.[8]

Parallel findings emerge from studies of moral identity and behavior. In a study of highly committed moral exemplars, William Damon and I found that many of these individuals did not exhibit the exceptional commitment that came to characterize their lives until well into adulthood.[9] For example, we wrote about a woman who was a self-described racist into her thirties who became a leader in the black civil rights movement in her late thirties and early forties through a series of transformative experiences that took place over several years. Similarly, we described a businessman who was financially successful, but rather unremarkable from the moral point of view, who became a tireless advocate for the poor in middle age, establishing and devoting much of his time and energy to a program that provides a broad range of services to low-income people in the Roanoke Valley of Virginia.

8. A. Colby, L. Kohlberg, J. Gibbs and M. Lieberman, "A Longitudinal Study of Moral Judgment," *Monographs of the Society for Research in Child Development* 48:1–2 (1983). J. Rest, D. Narvaez, M. Bebeau, and S. Thoma, *Postconventional Moral Thinking* (Mahwah, N.J.: Lawrence Erlbaum, 1999).

9. A. Colby and W. Damon, *Some Do Care: Contemporary Lives of Moral Commitment* (New York: Free Press, 1992).

Even if it is possible for people to develop morally in adulthood, some would say that it is presumptuous for institutions of higher education to try to affect the moral understanding and behavior of adult students. In response to this objection, I ask whether it is presumptuous to help undergraduate students think more clearly about challenging moral dilemmas, engage in an intellectually serious way the moral issues that arise in academic disciplines, and participate in service to the community, reflecting on what is learned in the process. And is it presumptuous to ask them to adhere to high ethical standards regarding academic integrity and other issues of honesty and mutual respect within the campus community, become interested in and knowledgeable about contemporary social, policy, and political issues, participate in public discourse and debate regarding campus and community issues, and take advantage of opportunities to act on their most cherished beliefs? Understood in this way, it would seem that moral and civic education is appropriate not only to adults who are attending college but to all adults. Public lectures, community forums, public radio and television, church and political party membership, cultural events such as theater and museum exhibits, self-help groups such as Alcoholics Anonymous, and interest groups that discuss books and films all provide continuing opportunities for moral and civic growth for adults who are well past their college years. I would go so far as to argue that every institution of society that attempts to deepen individual and collective understanding, including the media, religion, and the arts, has a responsibility to foster moral and civic learning.

Argument: College Students Are Primarily Consumers of Vocational Training

Another objection to undergraduate moral and civic education derives from the tendency discussed earlier to see higher education as a commodity purchased by students as an investment in their future earning power. The argument is that students are consumers who want to buy occupational preparation, not moral and civic education. It is true that students (and their parents) consider career preparation the primary purpose of their undergraduate education, even at small liberal arts colleges.[10] Moreover, the overwhelming majority of undergraduates major in a particular discipline because they believe it provides the quickest, safest route to highly paid employment, which has made business the number one major at American colleges and universities. Clearly, vocational preparation is a valid and important goal of higher education, but vocational preparation need not compete with or be disconnected from other goals. Institutions of higher education are well-situated to encourage students to think about a vocation as something larger and potentially far richer than simple careerism. The special nature of colleges and universities as intellectual communities gives them opportunities to embed the occupational goals of students in a broader and more socially meaningful framework.

Vocational preparation should not be treated as an endeavor that is distinct from growth in moral and civic responsibility. Work is central to the lives of most adults, a primary domain in which we have the opportunity to contribute to the welfare of others or to the community more broadly. Work is also one of the two or three most important places where we seek meaning in our lives.[11] For these reasons, it is important to integrate into any educational program a concern for ethical and socially responsible occupational practices and to place students' understanding of their occupation in a larger social and intellectual context for deeper meaning. In effect, higher education can help turn occupations into callings, and they will be better for it.

10. R. H. Hersh and D. Yankelovich, "Intentions and Perceptions: A National Survey of Public Attitudes toward Liberal Arts Education," *Change* 29:2(1997): 16–23.

11. A. Colby, L. Sippola, and E. Phelps, "Social Responsibility and Paid Work in Contemporary American Life," in A. Ross, ed., *Caring and Doing for Others: Social Responsibility in the Domains of Family, Work, and Community* (Chicago: University of Chicago Press, in press).

Argument: Moral and Civic Education Are Intellectually Weak

A question often raised about undergraduate moral and civic education is whether academic learning suffers if faculty broaden their educational goals in this way. If it is to be effective, this work must be intellectually rigorous and programmatically powerful. In our investigations of curricular and extracurricular programs of moral and civic education, we see many that meet the highest standards of quality. As in other areas of higher education, we also see weak programs. To ensure that this uneven quality does not short-change and alienate students or detract from the credibility of the enterprise, programs of moral and civic education need tough-minded scrutiny even when their goals are unimpeachable. We also need to develop creative tools for assessment research to demonstrate good programs' quality to the range of interested publics and provide the kind of information that will improve ineffective programs.

We believe that this research can demonstrate that the best programs actually have a positive impact on academic learning as well as on moral and civic responsibility. In an evaluation of a large number of service learning programs, Alexander Astin and his colleagues found significant positive effects of participation in service-learning on grade point average, writing skills, and critical thinking skills, as well as commitment to community service, self-efficacy, and leadership ability.[12] Eyler and Giles report research indicating that students' academic performance and self-assessment of their own learning and motivation increases through participation in high quality service-learning programs, especially those that involve challenging service work well in-

12. A. Astin, L. Vogelgesang, E. Ikeda, and J. Yee, "How Service Learning Affects Students: Executive Summary" (Los Angeles: Higher Education Research Institute, UCLA, January, 2000). Retrieved June 1, 2000, from *http://www.gseis.ucla.edu/slc/rhowas.html.*

tegrated with the course material and accompanied by opportunities for structured reflection on their service experience.[13] On the other hand, this research shows that the weaker service-learning experiences do not have these positive results. Clearly, quality matters, so we need to develop the tools both to evaluate and ensure the highest quality in all this work.

Conclusion

It is clear that students' values, moral and civic assumptions, and identities are shaped in college. It is time to be more self-conscious and intentional about this, and to think carefully about the particular framing of goals and strategies that are appropriate and feasible within a given institution. It is also important that faculty and administrators doing this kind of work document what they are doing and make it public so that it can be shared and discussed. This will open specific practices to critique and allow institutions to learn from their own and others' experience. Public scrutiny of these programs is a safeguard against practices that overstep the bounds of what is legitimate and will allow us to develop further the local and national discourse about what should be done and how best to accomplish it. This discourse can also help faculty and students think through dilemmas that arise in moral and civic education on college campuses, such as the tension between spirited debate and concern for others' feelings.

There are many approaches to fostering students' moral and civic responsibility in American higher education. Different conceptions of the goals and different programs of activity, both curricular and extracurricular, are appropriate to different kinds of institutions. A military academy will conceive of its specific goals quite differently from a community college on an Indian reservation; a nonresidential, public,

13. J. Eyler and D. Giles, *Where's the Learning in Service-Learning?* (San Francisco: Jossey-Bass, 1999).

urban university will have a very different approach from that of a small, religiously affiliated liberal arts college. It is important for each institution to build on the best of its own traditions and history as it creates new initiatives. In spite of this diversity, however, there are some common principles that underlie effective moral and civic education, and even institutions that are very different have a great deal to learn from each other.

First, the intellectual core of moral and civic development is critical. This includes not only critical thinking and the capacity to reason about moral and political issues in a sophisticated way (as described developmentally by Kohlberg and others), but also includes deep understanding of many content domains, including our political and economic systems, the fundamentals of ethical concepts in philosophy, and a grasp of American historical and cultural legacies as related to the global context. These are the traditional domains of a liberal arts education, with clear links to moral and civic development.

Second, educators must recognize that cognitive or intellectual dimensions cannot be separated from the dimensions of personal meaning, affect, and motivation in moral and civic education, or in general education. Any effort to focus on the narrowly intellectual alone is self-defeating because it does not result in lasting learning. Ideally, moral and civic education at the college level, as at younger ages, should take a holistic approach that affects the entire environment and its moral atmosphere, creating a campus climate among administration, faculty, and student peer culture that supports the education of the whole person around a core set of shared moral and intellectual concerns. This best ensures the development of routines of moral interpretation and habits of behavior grounded in trustworthiness, mutual respect, open-mindedness, concern for the welfare of others, and active, thoughtful citizenship.

A holistic, multi-faceted approach is especially conducive to creating an enduring identity that incorporates moral and civic concerns. We know this is the key to a strength of commitment that withstands the inevitable challenges that moral and civic engagement entail. In our study of moral exemplars who sustained exceptional levels of moral commitment over many decades, Bill Damon and I were interested to see that these people did not make sharp distinctions among their personal, professional, and moral goals. Instead, they defined themselves through their moral goals and fully integrated what they wanted personally with what they thought was right. Cabell Brand, the businessman who developed anti-poverty programs around Roanoke, Virginia, expressed his sense of moral and personal integration when I asked, "When you think about these moral goals and values and so on, how do these relate to your sense of who you are as a person?" He responded, "Well, it's one and the same. Who I am is what I'm able to do and how I feel all the time—each day, each moment . . . It's hard for me to separate who I am from what I want to do and what I am doing [in these programs]."[14] Mother Waddles, an African-American woman who established a mission for the low-income communities of Detroit, sounded remarkably like Brand, the wealthy white entrepreneur. In talking about the stability of her commitment to this work, she said, "Because I didn't promise that I would do it contingent upon what kind of building, what kind of clothes I could wear, what kind of money I had; just as long as I can find something I can do, I'll do it. So no matter where I am going, people can at least know to pinpoint me in what category I'm in. Without even asking, 'I know wherever she is, if she's alive and well, she's a missionary.' So I think that's my greatest achievement—to find yourself and know who you are, and get joy out of being you."[15]

People at this high level of commitment have found ways to integrate the things that inspire them and the things they want to accomplish and to build these into their core sense of who they are. This results not only in outstanding service to others but also in an exceptional degree

14. See Colby and Damon (1992): 304.
15. Ibid., 218.

of personal well-being and fulfillment for the exemplars themselves. Many people never achieve this level of personal integration. Developing a fully integrated life is one of the most challenging psychological tasks of adulthood. In older forms, which often began from a spiritual base and treated one's life work as a calling, this was accepted as a legitimate part of the agenda for higher education. It is now time to redefine this earlier vision in a contemporary framework and hold colleges and universities accountable for a fuller conception of the educated person.

Moral and Ethical Development in a Democratic Society

Irving Kristol

I HAVE BEEN asked to write about moral and ethical development in a democratic society, and I should like to express my discomfort with that term "development." It is such a curious word, so tantalizingly neutral and therefore so ambiguous in defining our relation to morality. After all, the title could easily have been "moral and ethical education in a democratic society." Why wasn't it? Well, I assume the reason is that we are not certain that it is a proper function of education to shape young people according to any specific set of moral standards, and the term "moral education" does imply an activity of that sort. Development, on the other hand, suggests that morality is something that exists embryonically within every child—rather like an intelligence quotient—and that education's purpose is to encourage it to unfold toward its fullest potential. Morality, in this view, is something that happens to one, so education then becomes a process of liberating human possibilities for this eventual happening rather than of defining human possibilities in an approved way.

This is certainly a very convenient notion for teachers or all those in a position of authority, because it means that they need not have any firm moral beliefs or provide a moral model of any kind. The process of development can then be regarded as a purely technical problem—of means, not of ends—and the solution is to get people, especially young people, to have feelings about morality and to think about it: to be morally sensitive and morally aware, as we say. Once this has been successfully accomplished, the task of education is finished. What kinds of people emerge from this process is something we can leave to the people themselves freely to decide; the final disposition of their moral sentiments and ideas is their business, not anyone else's.

It's all very odd and most interesting, rather as if an expert in gardening were to compose a manual on botanical development in a suburban landscape. He would give you all sorts of important information on how things grow—weeds as well as flowers, poison ivy as well as roses—without ever presuming to tell you whether you should favor one over the other, or *how* to favor one over the other. In fact, there are no such gardening manuals, precisely because any gardener has some definite ideas about how a garden might look. Different gardeners have different ideas, of course; but there is a limit to this variety. The idea of a garden does not, for instance, include an expanse of weeds or poison ivy, and no gardener would ever confuse a garden with a garbage dump.

In contrast, we seem unable or unwilling to establish defining limits to the idea of a moral person. We are, as it were, gardeners with all the latest implements and technology, but without an idea of a garden. Is this a function of mere ignorance? Or mere timidity? I think not. Rather, we have faith in the nature of people that we do not have in the botanical processes of nature itself, and I use the word "faith" in its full religious force. We really do believe that all human beings have a natural *telos* toward becoming flowers, not weeds or poison ivy, and that in the aggregate human beings have a natural predisposition to arrange themselves into gardens, not jungles or garbage heaps. This sublime and noble faith we may call the religion of liberal humanism. It is the dominant spiritual and intellectual orthodoxy in America today. Indeed, despite all our chatter about the separation of church and state, one can even say it is the official religion of American society today, compared wit which all other religions can be criticized as divisive and parochial. I happen not to be a believer in this religion of liberal humanism, but this is not the time or place for theological controversy and I am not, in any case, the best-qualified person for such a controversy. I shall simply remark on what I take to be a fact: Though the majority of the American people may well subscribe to some version of this religion—and I think they do—the young among us end up holding in contempt all the institutions in which the ethos of this religion is incarnated. Indeed, incredibly, they become increasingly alienated from these institutions, and end up feeling that these institutions are in some way unresponsive and irrelevant to their basic needs. Their parents soon echo these complaints.

The Legitimacy of Institutions

What I suggest is that the moral neutrality of our institutions, especially our educational institutions, robs them of their popular legitimacy. Nor does it matter if this moral neutrality is, at the moment, popularly approved of and sanctioned by public opinion. It still deprives these institutions of their legitimacy. One does not have to be a particularly keen student of history or psychology to know that people will accept, tolerate, or even praise institutions which later will suddenly be experienced as intolerable and unworthy. Institutions, like worm-eaten trees, can look healthy and imposing until they crumble overnight into the dust. If you look at the *cahiers* submitted to the French Assembly on the eve of the great revolution, you find not a breath of dissatisfaction with the monarchy—not a hint of republican aspirations. Similarly, early in 1964, an opinion poll among students at the University of California at Berkeley found that the overwhelming majority thought very well of the school and believed they were getting an excellent education there. Nevertheless, both Louis XVI and Clark Kerr soon found themselves riding the whirlwind. Such abrupt eruptions of profound discontent catch us all by surprise, whether we are talking about the rebelliousness of racial minorities, or young people, or women, or whomever. They are characteristic of American society today and also characteristic of a society whose institutions—whether they be political institutions, or schools, or the family—are being drained of their legitimacy—of their moral acceptance, for that is what legitimacy means.

We try to cope with this problem by incessantly restructuring our institutions to make them more responsive to popular agitation, but that obviously does not work very well. The more we fiddle around with our schools, the more energetically we restructure and then re-restructure them according to the passing fancy of intellectual fashion, the more steadily do they lose their good repute. One can only conclude that either there is something wrong with the idea of responsiveness as we currently understand it, or that there is some fault in our idea of the people as we currently understand it. I suggest that there is something wrong with both of these ideas as we currently understand them. Ultimately, we are talking about a single error rather than a dual one: an error in the way we conceive the relations between a people and their institutions in a democratic society.

Strategies of Responsiveness

There is an old Groucho Marx chestnut about how he resigned from a club immediately upon being elected to membership, his resignation prompted by the thought that any club that would elect him a member couldn't possibly be worth joining. I think that, in this old chestnut, there is a lesson for all of us about responsiveness. More and more of our institutions have been reaching out for greater participation and involvement, and an ever-larger number of those new recruits to full membership in the club have been busy resigning.

It is not easy to say to what degree our various strategies of responsiveness are motivated by sly cunning or plain self-deception. In the heyday of campus protest over the Vietnam war, amidst an upsurge of general political radicalism among college students, Congress decided to lower the voting age to eighteen. To the best of my knowledge, there was not a single protest meeting on any American campus on the issue of a lower voting age. Similarly, to the best of my knowledge, Congress did not receive a single mass petition on this matter from young people. Nevertheless, Congress decided that, in the face of unrest, it couldn't simply remain mute and impassive, so it decided to be responsive in its way. It didn't end the Vietnam war or abolish capitalism, but instead passed a constitutional amendment lowering the voting age to eighteen. That amendment was promptly ratified by the requisite number of state legislatures, and shortly thereafter Richard Nixon was elected President by an overwhelming majority of the popular vote.

One of the ways in which we characteristically respond is to give dissatisfied people what they have not asked for, what there was never any sound reason for believing they really wanted. Thus, when non-whites in the ghettos of New York City began to express dissatisfaction with the fact that their children graduated from high school without even being able to read or reckon at an elementary school level, they were promptly given community control over their local school boards and open admissions to the senior city colleges, but if you look back at the course of events, you will discover that there never was any real popular demand as distinct from political–demagogic demand for either community control or open admissions. Neither had any bearing on the problems at hand. As a matter of fact, any authentic conception of community control stood in rank contradiction to the practice of busing students for purposes of integration, which was also under way in New York's schools.

We are responsive in another seemingly more candid, but actually even more cunning, way. This is to give people what they actually demand—or what some vociferously demand—in the tranquil knowledge that because these demands are misconceived, their satisfaction is a meaningless gesture. That is what has happened with parietal rules, course gradings, class attendance, curriculum requirements, nominal student representation on various committees, and so forth, on so many of our college campuses, as well as in lower schools. The strategy may be defined as follows. When confronted with protest, dissatisfaction, and tumult, unburden yourself of your responsibilities but keep all your privileges, then announce that your institution has enlarged the scope of participation and freedom for all constituents. Since participation and freedom are known to be good democratic things, you have the appearance of rectitude and the reality of survival.

This complicated game of responsiveness has been skillfully played these past years and has enabled a great many institutions to secure their imperiled positions. In that sense, it has been unquestionably successful. In a deeper sense, however, it has gained nothing but time—a precious enough gain, but only if one realizes that it is simply time that has been gained, and that this time must be used productively if the gain is to be substantial rather than illusory. It is not my impression that any such realization exists.

Through the ages political philosophers and educators have argued that it is unwise to give people rights without, at the same time, imposing obligations—that rights without obligations make for irresponsibility, just as obligations without rights make for servility. Edmund Burke pushed this thesis further when he declared that it was part of the people's rights to have obligations—that an absence of obligation means a diminution of humanity because it signifies a condition of permanent immaturity. We can extend this line of thought even further and declare with confidence, based on our own more recent experience, that obligation is not only a right but a need. People upon whom no obligations are imposed will experience an acute sense of deprivation. It is our striking failure to recognize this phenomenon of moral deprivation for what it is that explains our fumbling, cynical response to the dissatisfaction that Americans express toward their institutions.

Institutions that pander to citizens (I use that word "pander" advisedly) in an effort to achieve popularity may get good press for a while. Our mass media, for which pandering is an economic necessity, are naturally keen to see other institutions remake themselves in the media's own image, to become responsive as a television station or network is responsive. Responsiveness here means to satisfy popular appetite or desire or whim or fancy or, rather, to satisfy what is thought at any moment to be popular appetite or desire or whim or fancy. Such responsiveness, being timely and circumstantial, is also thought to be relevant. But amidst the noise of mutual self-congratulation, what is lost sight of is the fact that these institutions, floating on clouds of approval and self-approval, have uprooted themselves from that solid ground of moral legitimacy from which all institutions receive their long-term nourishment.

Do I exaggerate? Well, let me cite the problems of ghetto education. During the past decades we have had dozens of bold innovations in the schooling of slum kids, each claiming to be more responsive and more relevant than the previous ones. Some of these innovations have even revived forms of classroom organization and techniques of pedagogy that were popular a hundred years ago, and you can't be more innovative than that! Each innovation, at some moment, is held up as a breakthrough, is the subject of enthusiastic magazine articles and television reports, is quickly imitated by enterprising school administrators elsewhere, and is generally judged to be a success before any results are in. Then it quietly vanishes, and nothing more is heard about it as attention shifts to some later innovation, by some other bold educational reformer who has broken through encrusted tradition and has come up with an even more responsive and relevant program. Meanwhile, back in the ghetto, there exists a whole set of successful schools that no one pays any attention to—schools successful in the most elementary yet crucial terms: A long list of parents try desperately to register their children in these schools; the truancy and transfer rates are low, there is less juvenile delinquency and a lower rate of drug addiction among all students, and academic achievement levels tend to be slightly higher than average. I refer to the parochial schools in the ghetto, which no one writes about, which the media ignore, but which—in the opinion of parents and students alike—are the most desirable of all ghetto schools. Many of these parochial schools are in old buildings with minimal facilities—a pitiful library perhaps, a squalid gymnasium perhaps, a Spartan lunchroom perhaps. Anyone who ever takes the trouble to open his or her eyes to the existence of these schools is not taken aback—as so many were—by the findings of the Coleman report that the condition or even nonexistence of such physical facilities had little connection with educational achievement.

Why are the parochial schools in the ghetto so well regarded? The answer is obvious: They are self-respecting institutions, demanding institutions, with standards that students are expected to meet. Many of them enforce dress codes as a symbolic gesture of self-affirmation. By making such demands upon their students, they cause them to make demands upon themselves and, most important, cause their students to realize that the only true moral and intellectual "development" occurs when you do make demands upon yourself.

The Case for Authority

I suppose that what I am saying can and will be interpreted as just another critique of what we call permissiveness. I should be unhappy if this happens, because I so intensely dislike both that term and its associations. People who indiscriminately attack permissiveness are themselves victims of confusion between authority and authoritarianism—a confusion they share with the very tendencies they criticize. Permissiveness and authoritarianism are two possible poles of moral discourse. Both of them are poles that come into existence when the center no longer holds. That center is authority, meaning the exercise of power toward some morally affirmed end in such a reasonable way as to secure popular acceptance. Legitimate authority is not always reasonable, since it is exercised by people who are not always naturally reasonable. No one is always reasonable, and therefore legitimate authority is open to criticism and correction. But if authority may be flawed in operation, both permissiveness and authoritarianism are flawed in their morally void and substanceless goals. This second flaw is clearly infinitely more important than the first. It induces a kind of technocratic mania, with exponents of permissiveness devising ever-new ways of liberating the citizen, with no idea as to what he is being liberated for, while exponents of authoritarianism are busy learning how to control people solely to secure the power of existing institutions, with no serious conception about the ultimate purpose of this power.

Properly understood, authority is to be distinguished from power, which is the capacity to coerce. In the case of authority, power is not experienced as coercive because it is infused, however dimly, with a moral intention that corresponds to the moral sentiments and moral ideals of those who are subject to this power. Education, in its only significant sense, is such an exercise in legitimate authority. When educators say that they don't know what their moral intention is, that they don't know what kinds of human beings they are trying to create, they have surrendered all claim to legitimate authority. Moral development, as now conceived in our schools of education, is never associated with ultimate mental intentions. (That would be authoritarian.) As a result, what we call moral development can easily give rise to moral deprivation—a hunger of the soul for moral meanings—which is far more devastating and dangerous than physical hunger. In the end, this hunger of the soul will satisfy itself by gratefully submitting to any passing pseudoauthority. But where on earth, in this bewildered age, are our educators going to discover this moral authority without which authentic education is impossible? Who is going to answer questions about the meaning of our individual and collective lives? I recognize both the cogency and poignancy of this lament: Ours is indeed a bewildered age. I would say this: If you have no sense of moral authority, if you have no sovereign ideas about moral purpose, you ought not to be educators. There are many technocratic professions in which, for all practical purposes, the knowledge of means suffices, but education is not one of them. An educator who cannot give at least a tentative, minimally coherent reply to the question, "Education for what?" and who cannot at least point to the kinds of persons a good education is supposed to produce, is simply in the wrong line of work. It is my impression that, in fact, most educators, being sincerely committed to the educational enterprise, are in the right kind of work. Most do know more than they feel free to admit about the aim of education to achieve this freedom as one of the major purposes of education reform today.

Contributors

MARVIN W. BERKOWITZ, Sanford N. McDonnell Professor of Character Education at the University of Missouri-St. Louis, has served as Ambassador Holland H. Coors Professor of Character Development at the United States Air Force Academy and professor of psychology and founder and director of the Center for Ethics Studies at Marquette University. He is a developmental psychologist interested in child and adolescent development, moral thinking, and character education, with special interests in moral conflict discussion, adolescent risk-taking, parenting, and substance abuse.

ANNE COLBY joined the Carnegie Foundation for the Advancement of Teaching as a senior scholar in 1997. Prior to that, she was director of the Henry Murray Research Center at Harvard University, a longitudinal studies data archive and social science research center. She is the principal author of *A Longitudinal Study of Moral Judgment* (1983) and *The Measurement of Moral Judgment* (1987), co-author with William Damon of *Some Do Care: Contemporary Lives of Moral Commitment*

(1992), and coeditor of *Ethnography and Human Development: Context and Meaning in Human Inquiry (1995)*, and *Competence and Character through Life* (1998). At the Carnegie Foundation, she is codirector of the Preparation for the Professions Program and the Project on Higher Education and the Development of Moral and Civic Responsibility.

WILLIAM DAMON is Professor of Education and Director of the Center on Adolescence at Stanford University. He received his Ph.D. in developmental psychology from University of California at Berkeley. Damon's books include *Self-understanding in Childhood and Adolescence* (1988); *The Moral Child* (1990); *Some Do Care: Contemporary Lives of Moral Commitment* (1992); *Greater Expectations* (1995); and, most recently, *The Youth Charter: How Communities Can Work Together to Raise Standards for All Our Children* (1997). Damon is editor-in-chief of *New Directions for Child Development* and *The Handbook of Child Psychology*. He has been elected to membership in the National Academy of Education. Damon is a Hoover Institution senior fellow.

AMITAI ETZIONI is the first university professor of The George Washington University. He is the author of twenty-one books, including *The Monochrome Society* (Princeton: Princeton University Press, April 2001), *Next: The Road to the Good Society* (New York: Basic Books, January 2001), *The Limits of Privacy* (New York: Basic Books, Spring 1999), and *The New Golden Rule: Community and Morality in a Democratic Society* (New York: Basic Books, 1996), which received the Simon Wiesenthal Center's 1997 Tolerance Book Award. He is also editor of *The Responsive Community: Rights and Responsibilities*, a communitarian quarterly.

IRVING KRISTOL is coeditor of *The Public Interest* magazine, John M. Olin Distinguished Fellow at the American Enterprise Institute, a fellow of the American Academy of Arts and Sciences, and a lifetime member of the Council on Foreign Relations. He is the author of *Neoconservatism: The Autobiography of an Idea* (1995), *Reflections of a*

Neoconservative (1983), *Two Cheers for Capitalism* (1978), and *On the Democratic Idea in America* (1972).

F. CLARK POWER is a professor in the Program of Liberal Studies, concurrent professor of psychology, and fellow of the Institute for Educational Initiatives at the University of Notre Dame. He also serves as the associate director for academic affairs and research for the Mendelson Center for Sports, Character, and Culture. He received an Ed.D. in Human Development from Harvard's Graduate School of Education in 1979. His research and writing focus on moral development and democratic education. He is a coauthor of *The Measurement of Moral Judgment, Vol. II: Standard Issue Scoring Manual*, and *Lawrence Kohlberg's Approach to Moral Education*; he is also coeditor of *Self, Ego and Identity: Integrative Approaches*; *The Challenge of Pluralism: Education, Politics and Values*; and *Character Psychology and Character Education* (forthcoming).

ARTHUR J. SCHWARTZ has directed the character development programs for the John Templeton Foundation since 1995. He also serves as project director for the Foundation's popular guidebook *Colleges That Encourage Character Development*. He received his doctorate from Harvard University.

NANCY SHERMAN is university professor of philosophy at Georgetown University. In 1997–99, she served as the inaugural holder of the Distinguished Chair in Ethics at the United States Naval Academy. She has been an associate professor of philosophy at Yale University and has held visiting positions at Johns Hopkins and the University of Maryland. She is the author of *The Fabric of Character* (Oxford University Press, 1989) and *Making a Necessity of Virtue* (Cambridge University Press, 1997) and the editor of *Critical Essays on the Classics: Aristotle's* Ethics (Rowman and Littlefield, 1999). She has written over thirty published articles in the general area of ethics and moral psychology. Professor Sherman holds a Ph.D. from Harvard University in philosophy (1982).

CHRISTINA HOFF SOMMERS is a resident scholar at the American Enterprise Institute in Washington, D.C. She is the author of *The War Against Boys* and *Who Stole Feminism?*

LAWRENCE J. WALKER is professor of psychology and coordinator of the graduate program at the University of British Columbia, having received his Ph.D. from the University of Toronto in 1978. He is past president of the Association for Moral Education and currently serves as associate editor of the *Merrill-Palmer Quarterly*. His research focuses on issues relating to the psychology of moral development, including processes in the development of moral reasoning and the formation of moral personality.

Index